WITHSTANDING
THE ENEMY

DUNCAN CARR

McDougal Publishing is a ministry of The McDougal Foundation, Inc., a
Maryland nonprofit corporation dedicated to spreading the Gospel of the
Lord Jesus Christ to as many people as possible in the shortest time
possible.

Published by:
McDougal Publishing
P.O. Box 3595
Hagerstown, MD 21742-3595
www.mcdougal.org

ISBN 978-1-58158-114-0

Printed in the United States of America
For Worldwide Distribution

"Everyone who is called by My name, whom I have created for My glory; I have formed him, yes, I have made him." Isaiah 43:7

PREFACE

A model for intercessory prayer has been worked out to illustrate the steps that must be taken to develop and build up the faith needed to receive an answer to prayer.

> *Then he said to me, "Do not fear, Daniel, for from the first day that you set your heart to understand, and to humble yourself before your God, your words were heard; and I have come because of your words.*
> *"But the prince of the kingdom of Persia withstood me twenty-one days; and behold, Michael, one of the chief princes, came to help me, for I had been left alone there with the kings of Persia."*   Daniel 10:12 and 13

In the spiritual realm, as can be seen in Daniel chapter 10, there can be forces at work which can delay an answer to prayer—in this particular case the delay was twenty-one days. This illustration serves to remind us that we not only need the tools to develop faith, but we also need the persistence to maintain that faith. *Withstanding the Enemy* is a twenty-one day study demonstrating the practical biblical principles involved in receiving an answer to prayer by accessing the kingdom of God.

We have been created for the glory of God and have been called for the obtaining of the glory of the Lord Jesus Christ for a reason. If Christ is formed in us, the Father can draw the unsaved to His Son. We need to ensure that we, as salt of the earth, do not lose our flavor as we go into the world. Just as Paul preached the kingdom of God, so must we, that we might be innocent of the blood of all men. May we sanctify the Lord God in our hearts and always be ready to give a defense to everyone who asks us the reason for our hope. May we abound in that hope by the power of the Holy Spirit.

CONTENTS

INTRODUCTION

If the foundations are destroyed, what can the righteous do?

During the late summer of 1973 I was afforded the opportunity to visit the Holy Land. A town that held particular significance was Tiberias, which provided a base from which a walk to Capernaum could be made—passing by Magdala and the Mount of the Beatitudes on the way.

At night in Tiberias many lights flickered in the distance all along the horizon on the other side of the Sea of Galilee on the Golan Heights. This was the Syrian army encampment preparing for the days to come. Taking advantage of an offer to cross the lake in a fishing boat, several of us made the trip. Within half an hour of our landing on the other side, the occupants of an Israeli army vehicle were advocating our withdrawal from what we were told was a Syrian minefield.

We survived our somewhat foolhardy adventure, and what happened in the next few weeks of 1973 is history. Despite overwhelming odds, why should we be surprised if God honors His promise that once Israel has returned to their land they will no longer be uprooted?

"I will bring back the captives of My people Israel; they shall build the waste cities and inhabit them; they shall plant vineyards and drink wine from them; they shall also make gardens and eat fruit from them. I will plant them in their land, and no longer shall they be pulled up from the land I have given them," says the LORD your God.　　Amos 9:14-15

This is how we should be approaching prayer—particularly intercessory prayer—in the face of overwhelming odds as the world views a particular situation. What is intercessory prayer? Intercessory prayer is that special kind of prayer in which we persist until we have the assurance that the answer is on the way. It may take a while to develop the faith necessary to look beyond the situation that our eyes can see or our ears can hear, but the greater truth is that we can walk by faith and not by sight.

It is the primary purpose of this book to share insights from the Word of God—the Holy Bible—concerning how to appropriate the kind of faith necessary for intercessory prayer. Anyone can pray a prayer and God may answer that prayer—but do we always get ourselves to that place where we know assuredly that the prayer is answered? There is a world of difference between believing God can answer a prayer and believing God has answered a prayer. That difference is faith, and the just must live by faith.

There is a remarkable promise in John 15:7: *"If you abide in Me, and My words abide in you, you will ask what you desire, and it shall be done for you* [you will have your answer to prayer]." We will look at what it means to abide in Him later, but for now we will focus on the very foundation—the Word of God. Colossians 3:16 instructs us to *"let the word of Christ dwell in* [us] *richly"*—but why is it so important that the Word abides in us? Second Timothy 3:16-17 tells us:

All Scripture is given by inspiration of God,

and is profitable for doctrine, for reproof, for correction, for instruction in righteousness, that the man of God may be complete, thoroughly equipped for every good work.

Why does the Word have such an effect? Is it not because it is living and powerful and takes effect when spoken? (see Hebrews 4:12, John 6:63, and Isaiah 55:10-11)

Some of us were raised in a culture that accepted the life and teachings of Christ as true but questioned some of the older scriptures, such as the flood of Noah's time. This was actually prophesied in 2 Peter 3:5-6.

For this they willfully forget: that by the word of God the heavens were of old, and the earth standing out of water and in the water, by which the world that then existed perished, being flooded with water.

In John 5:47, Jesus actually stated, *"If you do not believe his* [Moses'] *writings, how will you believe My words?"* Jesus Himself confirmed in Luke 20:37 that Moses wrote Exodus: *"But even*

Moses showed in the burning bush passage that the dead are raised, when he called the Lord...."

The subject of this book is prayer, particularly intercessory prayer. We have established that the Word of God must dwell in us, as it can be trusted implicitly as truth and has life in it to accomplish what God has spoken.

With regard to our prayer life, why else is it so important that the Word dwells in us? Is it not so that our faith can increase knowing we can pray according to His will? We are told in 1 John 5:14-15:

Now this is the confidence that we have in Him, that if we ask anything according to His will, He hears us. And if we know that He hears us, whatever we ask, we know that we have the petitions that we have asked of Him.

This is the second requirement of John 15:7, the verse with which we started our journey. We must pray according to the will of God, and the Word itself will reveal the will of God to us *in Him*.

Mark 11:24 says: *"Whatever things you ask*

when you pray, believe that you receive them, and you will have them." This is another promise which is related to John 15:7. The condition for receiving an answer to prayer is simply that we believe we have received the answer. Sometimes we do not have the faith we need in our prayer life.

The purpose of this study is to instruct on the sources of faith so that we can believe we receive the answer to prayer—because according to Mark 11, if that faith can be developed, we can have the answer. One of those sources of faith is the foundation itself—the living Word of God. According to Romans 10:17, *"Faith comes by hearing, and hearing by the word of God."* Notice that it is by hearing the Word that faith is developed—it is as if speaking the Word gives a special life to the Word. A prayer of two or more people in agreement will increase faith as the promises in the Word of God are proclaimed audibly.

Do we desire an answer to prayer? Do we desire the faith to receive that answer to prayer? Then let us build on the foundation that we have laid, trusting completely in the promises of the Word of God—for all the promises are yes and amen—*in Him* (see 2 Corinthians 1:20).

SOURCES OF FAITH

On some occasions we seize the opportunity to share the gospel of the kingdom of God with others, but at other times we fail. Why is this?

King David requested the presence of the Holy Spirit, that he might *"teach transgressors* [God's] *ways, and* [that] *sinners* [might] *be converted"* (Psalm 51:13). David had learned a lesson when he transgressed with Bathsheba, because the presence of God was not in Jerusalem with the ark of the covenant to guide him and convict him of sin at the time of his transgression. Uriah, on returning, confirmed that the ark of the covenant had been taken to the siege at Rabbah, and that he himself would not go down to his own house, because *"the ark and Israel and Judah are dwelling in tents"* (2 Samuel 11:11). The presence of God was between the cherubim on the ark. No wonder David prayed, *"Do not take*

Your Holy Spirit from me" (verse 11).

Jesus Himself was *"anointed"* by God *"to preach the gospel to the poor"* (Luke 4:18). If Jesus Himself needed to be anointed by the Spirit of the LORD to preach the gospel—how much more we need to be anointed in order to be effective. Is this not the essential difference between those occasions when we have the boldness to share the gospel and those occasions when we do not?

This study on prayer commenced with John 15:7, and we saw in the introduction that the Word needs to abide in us for three primary reasons.

1.   The Word does not return void.
2.   The Word confirms the will of God.
3.   The spoken Word generates faith.

Notice that if the second condition of John 15:7 is satisfied—namely, that we also abide *"in Him"*—then our guaranteed answer to prayer will glorify the Father and *"bear much fruit,"* which will include winning souls (see John 15:5 and 8). But what does it mean to be *"in Him"*?

First John 2:6 says, *"He who says he abides in Him ought himself also to walk just as He walked."* But these verses also explain how we know we are *"in Him."* Is it not to examine whether or not we keep His Word and have His love perfected in us? How do we know that the love of God has been perfected in us? (see 1 John 2:5) Is it not when we have no fear or concern having placed all our trust in Jesus Christ? (see 1 John 4:18)

When we get to a place where we have laid down our lives to the extent we fear nothing and have cast all of our cares on God, then it can be said that we are perfected in love. Our actions can no longer be manipulated by the world threatening us, as we have come to the point where we really don't care what the outcome is, knowing that it is God's will and all things work together for good. It might be a painful experience, but the wealth of learning gained is more than worth the price. We will obey His commandments. It is no accident that John 15:7-8 and John 15:16, which guarantee an answer to prayer, are separated by a verse like John 15:13, confirming that *"greater love has no one than this, than to lay down one's life for his friends"* is a death to all self-will and self-interest. We need to make room for the Holy Spirit in our lives and we do that by laying down our lives for others. We are commanded to *"believe on the name of His Son Jesus Christ and love one another"* (1 John 3:23). If this is done, the promise is that whatever we ask for we shall receive—because we keep His commandments.

First John 3:24 again confirms that *"he who keeps His commandments abides in Him."* Note also the instruction is not just to be *"in Him,"* but to abide *"in Him,"* which speaks of a continuing, unbroken state—not just on occasions when we need answers to prayer.

Notice also that 1 John 5:14-15, discussed in the introduction, does not say that if we ask according to His will, we have the petition—it says that *"...in Him, if we ask anything according to His will, He hears us."*

If we have fulfilled the two requirements of John 15:7, we have our answer—but how does this line up with Mark 11:24: *"Whatever things you ask when you pray, believe that you receive them, and you will have them?"*

In our prayer we can have only two possibilities—either we believe or we don't believe we have the answer. This is our starting point for a model of intercessory prayer. See Figure 1.

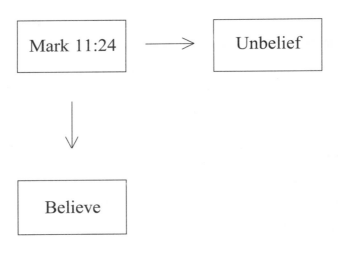

Figure 1

We need to answer the question, what is faith? Hebrews 11:1 states: *"Now faith is the substance of things hoped for, the evidence of things not seen."* Faith is not hoping that something will happen but knowing assuredly that something will happen. It has substance; it is the evidence or proof of things we cannot yet see. So when we pray, we need to answer the question, are we one hundred percent positive God has answered our prayer? Depending on our answer, our prayer path can go one of two different directions. See Figure 1.

What should we do if we believe, having assurance that our prayer is answered, but have not yet seen the promise with our eyes? Should we continue to pray? What should we pray? Clearly, we do not need to continue to ask for something we already have, yet have not seen. However, it is imperative we do not stop praying, or we risk losing the faith we have or we simply forget about the issue we've prayed about. By thanking God for His promises concerning this issue and continuing to abide in Him, we keep our faith until the answer is manifested.

In the account in Matthew 17:14-21 (see also Mark 9:14-29) the disciples failed to deliver the man's son because of unbelief. What was it that the disciples did not believe? Evidently they believed in deliverance, as there had been occasions when the disciples had delivered others, but this case was different. Romans 12:3 tells us that God *"has dealt to each one a measure of faith,"* and

Romans 12:6 instructs *"Having then gifts differing according to the grace that is given to us, let us use them."* If, in our daily walk, our faith is insufficient for us to believe in something, then clearly our faith needs to grow until it is sufficient. If we *"have faith as a mustard seed,"* as Matthew 17:20 states, we have the potential to move mountains. Jesus instructed His disciples that in order to appropriate the level of faith they needed, they needed to fast and pray. Fasting intensifies the anointing of God to increase our faith to believe and satisfy the requirement of Mark 11:24 that whatever we ask when we pray—if we believe it—we have it.

When the disciples asked Jesus to teach them to pray, His response was the Lord's Prayer, in Luke 11:1-4. The first request made of the Father in the Lord's Prayer is for the presence of the kingdom. Notice the similarity between this petition and the instruction given in Matthew 6:33 to *"seek first the kingdom"* and not to worry about our needs. If we need to pray *"Your kingdom come"* first of all and seek first His kingdom—what is the kingdom of God? Romans 14:17 tells us it is *"righteousness and peace and joy in the Holy*

Spirit." We need to be *"in Him"* to experience the kingdom in prayer, for the Holy Spirit is *"the Spirit of grace and supplication"* (Zechariah 12:10); *"the Spirit also helps in our weaknesses,"* and *"the Spirit Himself makes intercession for us"* (Romans 8:26).

Bearing in mind that the context is prayer, and an answer to the disciples' request to teach them to pray, Luke 11:5-8 tells us to persist in prayer until we have the answer. Does not this persistence maintain and increase our faith to believe in the promise of provision? This is further confirmed in the parable of the persistent widow seeking justice in Luke 18:1-8. What does verse 8 suggest is the purpose and result of our persistence in prayer when Jesus asks if the Son of Man will really find faith on earth when He comes? Does not this persistence maintain and increase our faith to believe in the promise of justice? The prayer is certainly not answered because God is wearied by our persistence. Does not the persistence of an anointed believer establish the kingdom of God more fully in the lives of men, so that even friends who have retired for the night and unbelieving judges are influenced by the presence of the anointing? We will speak more of this later.

Luke 11:9-13 continues the theme of persisting in prayer. We must ask, seek, and knock. What is the purpose of persistence? Is it not to increase the presence of the Holy Spirit in answering the prayer *"Your kingdom come,"* that we might truly be *"in Him,"* finding the faith we need and influencing the world around us—*"faith and love ... in Christ"* (1Timothy 1:14 and 2 Timothy 1:13). *"If you then, being evil, know how to give good gifts to your children, how much more will your heavenly Father give the Holy Spirit to those who ask Him!"* (Luke 11:13)

"And since we have the same spirit of faith, according to what is written, 'I believed and therefore I spoke,' we also believe and therefore speak" (2 Corinthians 4:13). Faith is in Christ. If we are truly *"in Him,"* we have a source of faith to help our prayer life. *"Now may the God of hope fill you with all joy and peace in believing, that you may abound in hope by the power of the Holy Spirit"* (Romans 15:13). In order to tap into that supernatural faith so our mustard seed of faith can grow, we must be *"in Him"* by our death to self-

will and self-interest. This is the greatest love, and the faith we so desperately need works through this love. *"For in Christ Jesus neither circumcision nor uncircumcision avails anything, but faith working through love"* (Galatians 5:6).

Doing as Jude 20 suggests, *"building yourselves up on your most holy faith, praying in the Holy Spirit,"* the conditions required to fulfill the promises of John 15:7-8 and Mark 11:24 may be realized. Remember that all the promises of God *"in Him"* are yes and amen.

Returning to Figure 1, the keys to overcoming unbelief can be represented very simply. As we have seen, faith can be developed by studying and hearing the Word of God as well as by ensuring that we are fully *"in Him"* by dying to self-interest. This is represented in Figure 2. If our first attempt to develop faith is unsuccessful, then we need the persistence to go around the loop as many times as is necessary to increase exposure to the Word of God and make more room for the infilling of the Spirit by death to self, so that the requirements of Mark 11:24 are fulfilled.

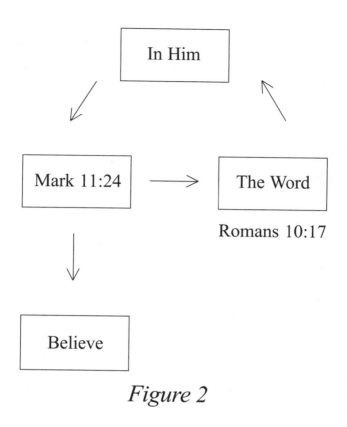

Figure 2

Day 2

ABIDING IN HIM

We need to believe God will use us as individuals to bring the gospel of the kingdom to others. No one can come to Christ unless the Father draws him—so if Christ is in us, then should we be surprised if we are picked out of a crowd as the Father draws someone to His Son? If we abide **in Him,** we ought to bear much fruit (see John 15:5). We have already seen that the key to being **in Him** is death to self. When the Greeks came asking to see Jesus, was not the instruction to be like a grain of wheat which if it dies will produce much grain? (see John 12:20-26) If we want to experience the Spirit of Christ today, why should it be any different for us?—He is *"the same yesterday, today, and forever"* (Hebrews 13:8). We surrender all things that we may be found **in Him,** that we may *"know Him and the power of His resurrection, and the fellowship of His sufferings, being conformed to His death"* (Philippians 3:10).

As we have already seen in 1 John 5:14, *"Now this is the confidence that we have in Him, that if we ask anything according to His will, He hears us."* It says that this is the confidence we have **in Him,** *"that if we ask anything according to His will, He hears us."* Likewise, 2 Corinthians 1:20 does not say that all the promises are yes and amen, but it says, *"All the promises of God **in Him** are Yes, and **in Him** Amen."*

John 15:7 says that we must *abide in Him* if our prayer is to be answered. It is not enough to be *"in Him"* only at the moment of salvation; we need to abide in Him continually. Colossians 2:6 says it another way: *"As you therefore have received Christ Jesus the Lord, so **walk in Him.**"* Verse 9 says, *"For in Him dwells all the fullness of the Godhead bodily."*

We have already seen in the previous chapter that we ought to **walk** as Jesus walked if the love of God is perfected in us and we are abiding **in Him** (see 1 John 2:5-6). First John 3:5-6 tells us that *"**in Him** there is no sin. Whoever **abides in Him** does not sin."* Is not the key **abiding in Him**? Clearly, abiding in Him denotes much more than being saved. It denotes a state that is so Spirit-filled that the very ground we walk on is holy: *"Building yourselves up on your most holy faith, praying in the Holy Spirit"* (Jude 20). It is only when *"the anointing that you have received from Him **abides** in you"* (1 John 2:27) that anyone **abides** in Him.

Jesus said, *"If you can believe, all things are possible to him who believes"* (Mark 9:23). We have only two options when we pray—either we believe it is done or we don't. If it is difficult to believe for a particular issue, then we need help. If we are not sure of the will of God in a particular situation, we need to be filled with the Spirit, and not with wine. These verses stress some of the requirements:

> *Therefore do not be unwise but understand what the will of the Lord is. And do not be drunk with wine, in which is dissipation; but be filled with the Spirit, speaking to one another in psalms and hymns and spiritual songs, singing and making melody in your heart to the Lord.* Ephesians 5:17-19

Moses as the writer of Genesis knew God as "Lord" [YHWH in original Hebrew](see Exodus 6:3). In Genesis 13:14-15 Abraham did not know God as "Lord" [YHWH]. Is it possible that Abraham, or Abram as he was called at that time, the father of faith, did not believe what God told him—namely, that he and his descendants would receive the land forever?

Moving forward to Genesis 15, we see in verses 2-6 that Abram prayed to the *"Lord God"* [Adonai YHWH in original Hebrew], and his faith that his descendants would be as many as the stars was accounted as righteousness. In Genesis 15:8 we note that he again prayed to the Lord God [Adonai YHWH] to get an answer. Abram asked how he would know he would inherit the land—so, clearly the father of faith had a problem believing, as the Lord had already told him two chapters earlier that he would receive it with his descendants. Abram sought his faith in Adonai—namely Jesus Christ, in whom are *"faith and love"* (1 Timothy 1:14). (See also Psalm 110:1, where *"the Lord* [YHWH] *said to my Lord* [Adonai] *'sit at my right hand' "*. Jesus Himself in Matthew 22:41-46 made it clear who Adonai is.)

Comparison of Matthew and Mark

"And as you go, preach, saying, 'The king-dom of heaven is at hand.' Heal the sick, cleanse the lepers, raise the dead, cast out demons. Freely you have received, freely give. Provide neither gold nor silver nor copper in your money belts, nor bag for your jour-ney, nor two tunics, nor sandals, nor staffs; for a worker is worthy of his food."

Matthew 10:7-10

And He called the twelve to Himself, and began to send them out two by two, and gave them power over unclean spirits. He com-manded them to take nothing for the journey except a staff—no bag, no bread, no copper in their money belts—but to wear sandals, and not to put on two tunics.

Mark 6:7-9

These are clearly two different occasions. Matthew's account was when faith was high (see

Matthew 9:35) and shoes and staffs were not required. Exodus 3:5 and Joshua 5:15 tell us that shoes need to be removed on holy ground. The topic of conversation was the kingdom of God. In Mark's account, faith was lacking (see Mark 6:5-6), shoes and staffs were called for, and only repentance was preached. It is also noteworthy that those with faith in Matthew 10:9 were told to provide no gold or silver or copper in their money belts, while those lacking faith in Mark 6:8 seemingly had only copper to leave behind.

"I am the Lord your God, who teaches you to profit, who leads you by the way you should go."   Isaiah 48:17

Just as the man Aaron was used by God and empowered by the rod to accomplish His purposes, so can we. In Psalm 23 David wrote: *"Your rod and Your staff, they comfort me."* Who is the Great Comforter but the Holy Spirit? In Micah 7:14 is written: *"Shepherd Your people with Your staff."* Isaiah 10:26-27 talks of God using His rod in the manner of Egypt and destroying the yoke because of the anointing oil. Truly, *"He who is in you is greater than he who is in the world"*

(1 John 4:4). It is our faith that overcomes the world (see 1 John 5:4).

Some of the things that hinder our abiding in Him and, consequently, receiving our answers to prayers are the absence of any of the following: unity (see Psalm 133, Matthew 18:19), forgiveness (see Mark 11:26), faith (see Mark 11:24, Acts 3:16, Jude 20), humility and brokenness (see Matthew 5:3), praise and thanksgiving (see Psalm 22:3 and Psalm 100), spiritual hunger (see Matthew 5:6, Ephesians 5:18), giving (see Psalm 76), protecting our faith, fasting and prayer (see Luke 5:33-39).

Developing our prayer model still further, we can include another two key verses reminding us of the promises of God as seen above. If we can truly get to the point where we are abiding in Him and His Word abides in us, then John 15:7 is fulfilled and we have the answer to our prayer. Even if we have to wait a little while for its manifestation, we know that the answer is on the way.

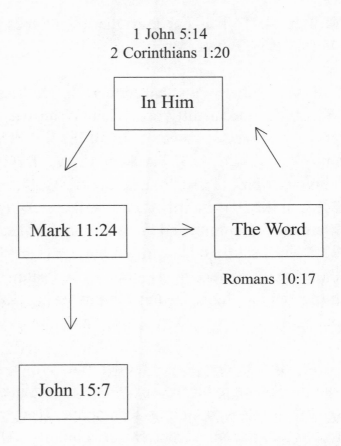

Figure 3

Day 3

PROTECTION OF FAITH

In the last chapter we saw Jesus give two different instructions to His disciples on two different occasions. When faith was high, all were healed and they preached the kingdom of God. Their lives were so filled with the Spirit of God that the ground itself became holy and sandals were removed. Their measure of faith had grown so much that they believed for healing and deliverance and did not need the staff. In the other account there was so much unbelief that they needed a staff—a turbocharge of kingdom power to overcome unbelief.

We have been taught to pray *"Your kingdom come"* when we start to pray, in Luke 11:2, and we have seen that the kingdom of God is *"righteousness and peace and joy in the Holy Spirit"* (Romans 14:17). We have been assured that we do not need to be concerned about our needs but to *"seek first the kingdom of God and His righteousness"* (Matthew 6:33). If our love abounds in all knowledge and discernment, then we will be filled with the fruits of His righteousness (see Philippians 1:9-11). The key is death to self in submission to others: Greater love has no man than this, that he lay down his life (see John 15:13). When the Spirit is poured out from on high, the effect of righteousness will be quietness and assurance forever (see Isaiah 32:15-17).

Then by our surrender to others we have assurance, which bolsters our faith. Remember Jude 20's instruction on how to build up faith, as we have already discussed. In Acts 3:11-16, the faith to heal the lame man at the gate came through Jesus Christ. We must remember that Jesus Christ is not only the author but also the finisher (or perfecter) of our faith (see Hebrews 12:1-2).

If we are truly *"in Him,"* if we are truly filled with the Spirit, our faith will be so high we will be like the group of disciples that Jesus sent out who did not need a staff. They had sought and found the kingdom and were preaching it. Remember the key to prayer is faith (see Mark 11:24) and our faith can grow through hearing the Word of God (see Romans 10:17) and by being *"in Him"* (see John 15:7).

It is important in prayer to ask according to His will. We have the promise that if *"in Him"* we ask according to His will, we have the answer (see 1 John 5:14-15)—but sometimes it is not clear what the will of God is in a given situation. Ephesians 5:17-21 provides the key to finding God's will. We need to be filled with the Spirit, which involves praise, thanksgiving, and submission to others—namely, death to self-interest. When the Greeks went to Philip and asked to see Jesus, it is not without significance that Jesus talked of a grain of wheat having to die to produce life. If we want to see Jesus and have His Spirit-filled life, we, too, must die to ourselves and the things of the world (see John 12:20-26).

Another key to accessing the kingdom of God and being covered with the oil of the anointing of the Spirit is unity in the body of Christ (see Psalm 133). Ephesians 4:16 states:

...from whom the whole body, joined and knit together by what every joint supplies, according to the effective working by which every

*part does its share, causes growth of the body
for the edifying of itself in love.*

In the Sermon on the Mount, Jesus talked of two groups of people who had ready access to the kingdom—namely, the poor in spirit and those who are persecuted for righteousness' sake.

Once we have accessed the kingdom, it is important to *abide in Him*—not just visit once in a while when the going gets tough. We need to be like the faith-filled disciples who needed no shoes, walking on holy ground, healing the sick, and saying that the kingdom has come near. In the account of the seventy who were sent out in Luke 10:1-9, why were they told to greet no one along the road? After all, weren't they supposed to be preaching the gospel of the kingdom? Was it not that they might be distracted from their purpose and start to question their faith? We must pray that the Lord will send out many more workers into the harvest field.

Both Isaiah 42:19 and John 9:39-41 speak of those who are blind being perfect and without sin. What does Jesus mean by these words? Clearly, those who do not see are the spiritually blind and they need to see and understand spiritual truth. But why must those who already see be made blind? Only those who *"abide in Him"* do not sin, so evidently these blind do not sin (see 1 John 3:5-6). Once we receive our spiritual sight, we must become blind to the lies that the world throws in our faces and trust in the greater truth of the promises of God. Did not Jesus say, "I am the way, the truth and the life?" (see John 14:6)

The key is to continually *"abide in Him"* and not be distracted, so that faith is protected and will not disappear. If the promise of God is prayed, it is done as long as we are *"in Him"* (see 2 Corinthians 1:20). We must get to the place where we ignore what our eyes see and what our ears hear, for the truth of the gospel of the kingdom is greater.

In Matthew 9:27-31, Jesus told the two blind men that their healing was according to their faith, but He warned them not to tell anyone. They ignored Him. Moving forward eleven chapters in the same gospel, to Matthew 20:29-34, the consequence of their disobedience appears to be that they lost their sight again. Could it be that this was a result of doubts about their healing being planted by those with whom they talked?

The city of Bethsaida was a city of unbelief, according to Matthew 11:21. It is interesting to note that in Mark 8:22-26, Jesus' first step before healing this man was to get the man away from this town. Notice that unbelief still gripped this man to some degree, as he saw men like trees. Note that Jesus made him act in faith by asking him to look up. Again, Jesus warned him not to go back into the town—presumably because the unbelief there would destroy his new found faith.

Day 4

THE MIND OF CHRIST

We as Christians need to regularly examine our-selves to see if our spiritual development is all that it should be—not that we can do anything ourselves but be yielded to the leading of the Holy Spirit, but where is our hunger level? After all, *"eye has not seen nor ear heard"* what God has in store for His people (see 1 Corinthians 2:9). Our experience of God is probably a small frac-tion of what God desires us to have. Let us move on from elementary principles and partake of solid food (see Hebrews 5:14-6:3).

I beseech you therefore, brethren, by the mer-cies of God, that you present your bodies a living sacrifice, holy, acceptable to God, which is your reasonable service. And do not be conformed to this world, but be trans-formed by the renewing of your mind, that you may prove what is that good and accept-

able and perfect will of God.

Romans 12:1-2

Romans 12:1-2 tells us that we need to be trans-
formed by the renewing of our minds, that we
might prove what is that good and acceptable and
perfect will of God. To "prove" something is in
the sense of proving a case in a court of law. How
do we prove the will of God by having our minds
transformed?

Yes, as believers we need to guard what we
think about—we are exhorted elsewhere to think
upon positive things (see Philippians 4:8). However, in the context of Romans 12, it is much more
than being careful what we allow ourselves to
think about. Romans 12:3-8 tells us that God has
given each one of us a measure of faith and He
expects us to use the gifts He has given us in pro-
portion to our faith. He expects that faith to grow.
In being transformed by the renewing of the mind,
we must start believing what God has told us He
will do rather than what the world is telling us or
what our physical eyes may be seeing. God's
promises are more real than the world and we need
to believe Him. We can prove, or demonstrate,
His will by believing His will in our minds as well

as in our hearts. Then, according to His promise, whatever things we ask for when we pray—believing, we shall receive them.

In the previous chapter we talked about the importance of protecting our faith. Philippians 4:6-7 tells us how to guard our hearts and our minds through Christ Jesus with the supernatural peace of God. If we make known our requests to God with thanksgiving rather than worrying about how we are to fix a problem, then we do not allow the negativity of the world to affect our faith or concern ourselves with our own shortcomings.

It is possible to have great peace of mind in a particularly bad situation by trusting what God's Word says in verses such as Romans 8:28: *"And we know that all things work together for good to those who love God, to those who are the called according to His purpose."* However, we must not make the mistake of accepting that a bad situation is the perfect will of God—we still need to persist in prayer until we are delivered from whatever situation we find ourselves in. God might allow us to go through some painful experience to educate us in a divine principle, but it is not

His perfect will that we stay there, even if His peace that surpasses all understanding has removed all anxiety concerning the situation.

The gates of hell cannot resist the church (see Matthew 16:18-19 and Genesis 22:17-18). Gates are defensive, but we need to go on the offensive spiritually. We will speak more of the importance of the words we speak at a later time. Here we will focus on what we think in the mind.

According to 2 Corinthians 10:4-6, the weapons of our warfare are mighty in God for casting down arguments and bringing every thought into captivity. We need to remember that we do not wrestle against flesh and blood, but against spiritual principalities and powers, and therefore must pray with all prayer and supplication in the Spirit, wearing the whole armor of God (see Ephesians 6:10-18). In waging spiritual warfare, we need to abide by certain rules of engagement outlined in the Word of God. When an anointed person moves to a new area, demons react (see Mark 5:2). Demons are territorial and fearful of being tormented themselves (see Mark 5:7-10). They do not want to move away from the country where they have become established. There is a reason why Jesus commanded His disciples to stay in the same house when He sent them out (see Mark 6:10-13). The weapons of our warfare are mighty for casting down arguments and bringing every thought into captivity, but we don't want the weapons blunted by having to fight unnecessary battles if we frequently move from house to house.

We must beware and be aware of spirits of idolatry that are stirred up when the Holy Spirit is present. The people in the wilderness sacrificed to the idol they had created, despite the glory on Moses and the daily presence of the pillar of cloud and the manna. They not only sacrificed to the God of Israel but also worshipped an idol (see Acts 7:40-43). In places where God's Spirit has been poured out, spirits of idolatry will compete for the territory. The hill of God must not become a Philistine garrison (see 1 Samuel 10:5). The Philistines attacked when they heard of David's anointing, but because David went to the stronghold and inquired of the LORD, they were defeated and had to leave their idols behind (see 2 Samuel 5:17-21).

When the water came from the rock, Amalek ambushed Israel (see Exodus 17:5-8). Saul was sent to utterly destroy Amalek because of this event, but he disobeyed (see 1 Samuel 15:1-9). Samuel rebuked Saul, telling him that *"to obey is better than sacrifice,"* but *"rebellion is as the sin of witchcraft, and stubbornness is as iniquity and idolatry"* (see 1 Samuel 15:22-23). At the encounter with the rock, it was because of the rebellion of the people against God's Spirit that Moses spoke rashly with his lips (see Psalm 106:32-33).

When Jesus taught the people to labor for the food which endures to everlasting life, they asked how. He responded that they were to believe (trust) in Him (Jesus) who was sent (see John 6:27-29). We have already seen how we must protect our faith from being destroyed by a world of unbelief. We saw the story of the two blind men in Matthew 9 who were healed according to their faith and told not to tell anyone; eleven chapters later we hear of two blind men again. We briefly touched on the story of the blind man at Bethsaida who after being healed was told not to go into the city again (see Mark 8:22-26).

In this chapter we will move on from a discussion of how to increase and protect our faith by spiritually feeding and protecting our minds and talk of John the Baptist. In Luke 1:15 we hear that John was to be filled with the Holy Spirit even from his mother's womb. However, in Matthew 11:11, Jesus stated that even though there was none greater than John born of a woman, he who was least in the kingdom of heaven was greater than John. How was this possible? The implication was that John could not access the kingdom as a man.

We need to clearly understand what Matthew understood about the kingdom of God. We need to remember that the kingdom is righteousness, peace, and joy in the Holy Spirit (see Romans 14:17), and that the kingdom of God is not in word but in power (see 1 Corinthians 4:20).

In Matthew 11:2-3 we see John in prison with his faith seemingly shaken. The man who had introduced the Messiah to his own disciples as the Lamb of God who takes away the sin of the world in John 1:29 now asked if Jesus was the Coming One. We have seen how faith can be appropriated spiritually. We have seen how, in Acts 3:16, the man was healed at the Beautiful Gate through the faith which comes through Jesus. In Jude 20 we have heard about the importance of a faith that can be built up. Seemingly, even though John was filled with the Spirit from his mother's womb, he wasn't able to access that same source of faith.

Hebrews 8:5 tells us that the earthly tabernacle created in Moses' time was a copy of the heavenly tabernacle. Hebrews 4:16 exhorts us to come boldly to the throne of grace to obtain mercy and grace to help in time of need. The throne of grace is therefore in the heavenly Holy of Holies where we find the very presence of God, and access to this sacred location was denied until Calvary (see Hebrews 9:8).

It is the blood of Jesus and union with the Spirit (His flesh) that allows us to boldly enter into the Holy of Holies in full assurance of faith (see Hebrews 10:19-22). *"It is the Spirit who gives life; the flesh profits nothing. The words that I speak to you are spirit, and they are life"* (John 6:63).

First Corinthians 6:17 tells us that if we are

joined to the Lord, we are one spirit with Him. Ephesians 2:18 tells us that through Him we have access by one Spirit to the Father.

Second Corinthians 3:7-18 tells us that the glory of the Old Covenant under Moses pales into insignificance compared with the glory of the New Covenant which we can experience. John could not access the heavenly Holy of Holies despite being filled with the Spirit from birth. Therefore, he who is least in the kingdom accessing the Holy of Holies, being one spirit with the Lord, is greater than John.

Colossians 2:9 teaches us that *"in Him dwells all the fullness of the Godhead bodily."* What a privilege we have as believers to be able to enter into the presence of the Father Himself— yet, sadly, so many are content to be lukewarm and stay in the outer courts, thinking they have found the throne of grace. Only those who enter the inner sanctuary—the spiritual Holy of Holies—can access the kingdom of God and the true glory of the New Covenant. Even the least of these has more access to the presence of God than John the Baptist had.

The context of John 9:35-10:10 is believing (trusting) in the Son of God—not just being blind to the things of the world which are in contradiction to the Word of God, but also entering the sheepfold by Christ, that we might not only be saved but have life more abundantly.

Day 5

ELIJAH AND ELISHA

We saw that the least in the kingdom was greater than John the Baptist even though he was filled with the Spirit from the womb and he was the greatest prophet born of a woman.

We have seen Jesus' instruction to seek first the kingdom and pray, *"Thy kingdom come."* For further confirmation that Jesus is talking of a kingdom of power that is accessible to us now, let us continue.

In Matthew 16:28-17:1, Jesus ascended the Mount of Transfiguration six days after saying that some would see the Son of Man coming in His kingdom. In Mark 9:1-2, the Scriptures say that Jesus ascended the mountain six days after saying that some standing with Him would see the kingdom present with power. The reason they went up the mountain was to pray (see Luke 9:27-28). However, these same verses reveal that Jesus took His disciples up the mountain about eight days after saying that some standing with Him would SEE the kingdom.

Clearly, there will be a day when Christ returns to earth when He comes in His kingdom, which will then be present with power. However, true believers worshiping in spirit and truth will see His kingdom before His return. What then is the significance of His saying that they will see the kingdom two days before He talks of His return? Could this correspond to the words of Peter when he told his readers not to forget that with the Lord one day is as a thousand years, suggesting a gap of two thousand years between first seeing the kingdom and seeing the Son of Man coming again? (see 2 Peter 3:8)

In the Old Testament there are some interesting observations about the lives of Elijah and Elisha which point to the New Testament believer. The angel foretold that John would go before Jesus in the spirit and power of Elijah (see Luke 1:17). Elijah and John even dressed in a similar fashion (see 2 Kings 1:8 and Mark 1:6).

Just as John preceded Christ, Elijah preceded Elisha. It is of significance that the name *Elijah* means "God is Jehovah," whereas the name *Elisha* means "God is salvation." When the lawyer asked how to inherit eternal life, Jesus made it clear that the law provided the answer—namely, loving God with all his being and loving his neighbor (see Luke 10:25-28).

It is probably also of some significance that Elisha requested and received a double portion of the spirit that was upon Elijah (see 2 Kings 2:8-12). We will talk more of that significance at a later time. Several things about Elisha's ministry point directly to Christ: for example, his delegation of tasks to others. When he fed the one hundred with twenty loaves of bread, he delegated the task as Jesus did when He fed the five thousand (see 2 Kings 4:42-44 and Matthew 14:19). When he healed Naaman, again Elisha delegated a messenger to convey instructions on washing in the Jordan (see 2 Kings 5:9-11). In a similar way, Jesus delegated to His disciples the authority to baptize in the Jordan (see John 4:1-2). Jesus also delegated to His disciples when He instructed them to go and make more disciples, and He has promised that He will continue to work with us (see Matthew 28:19-20 and Mark 16:20).

The ministry of Elisha was representative of the New Covenant. Both Elijah and Elisha encountered a widow. In Elijah's encounter, she needed flour and oil to bake bread to survive, which points to the Old Covenant of the word of the law and the anointing. Neither the flour nor the oil ran out until the drought ended (see 1 Kings 17:8-16). In Elisha's encounter, the widow had nothing but oil—but that was sufficient as long as the oil was being used to fill vessels. Does this not point to the New Covenant, when we have the anointing abiding in us, not needing that anyone should teach us, as the Word dwells in our hearts through faith? (see 1 John 2:27) The widow's oil could be sold to pay debts and to provide for her sons and herself (see 2 Kings 4:1-7). Is it not the vessels full of oil that were set apart? (see verse 4) Were not the foolish virgins lacking oil told to go and buy some? (see Matthew 25:1-13)

There is a faith lesson of prayer in the story of the raising of the Shunammite's son from the dead (see 2 Kings 4:17-37). When her husband asked why she was going to the man of God, the woman said, "It is well," despite the fact that the child had already died (see verse 23). She said exactly the same thing to Gehazi in verse 26 when he asked about the welfare of the child. In these circumstances there was no opportunity for any negative words from her husband or from Gehazi to dampen her faith. We need to remember the words of Paul, who reminds us that He who supplies the Spirit and works miracles among us does it by the hearing of faith (see Galatians 3:5). When Jesus was on the way to heal Jairus' daughter, His instruction to Jairus was to *"only believe"* (Mark 5:35-36). The instruction to Gehazi in 2 Kings 4: 29 to take a staff and greet no one along the road is one repeated to New Testament disciples, as already discussed in an earlier chapter.

Day 6

FASTING

In all cases, fasting should be discussed with a medical professional before a fast is started.

The Old Testament speaks of designated fasts, for example, the Day of Atonement and the fasts outlined in Zechariah 8:19. There are different types of fasts ranging from total fasts to partial fasts. Total fasts—forsaking all food and drink— are exemplified by Moses' forty days on the mountain in Exodus 34:28, Paul's three-day fast after his Damascus road experience in Acts 9:9, and Esther's three-day fast in Esther 4:16. When the people of Nineveh repented at Jonah's preaching, the king issued a decree that not just the people but also the animals undertake a total fast in Jonah 3:5-9.

There are partial fasts as exemplified in Daniel 10:2-3, when Daniel ate no desirable or pleasant food for three weeks.

Isaiah 58:5-9 outlines the purpose of a fast. A fast is a time of self-examination (afflicting the soul) and of humbling oneself before God. The purpose of a fast is to loose the bonds of wickedness, to undo heavy burdens, to let the oppressed go free, and to break every yoke. We need to remember the underprivileged and provide for them. Then the very presence of God will rest upon us—healing will come speedily and the glory of God will be our rear guard. The anointing of the Holy Spirit will rest upon us and break every yoke (see Isaiah 10:27). The anointing oil speaks of the Holy Spirit. Fasting brings a greater presence of the Spirit of God. *"The Lord is the Spirit, and where the Spirit of the Lord is, there is liberty"* (2 Corinthians 3:17). *"If the Son makes you free, you shall be free indeed"* (John 8:36). Jesus was anointed *"to proclaim liberty to the captives"* (Luke 4:18).

Matthew 9:14-17 and Luke 5:36-39 speak of the need for new wine to be put into new wineskins. The new wine speaks of the Holy Spirit. Jesus answers the disciples' question about fasting by saying that their vessels will have to be renewed (born again) to be filled with the new wine of the Holy Spirit. These scriptures also point to a double portion of the anointing—the outer garment or mantle that is worn as a covering in addition to the wine, which is taken internally. More will be said about this later—for now, the discussion is about fasting.

Another purpose of fasting is to manifest God's promises. When Jehoshaphat was outnumbered by the enemy in 2 Chronicles 20:1-3, he proclaimed a fast throughout all Judah. He prayed in the house of the Lord that if disaster came upon them, that God would hear and save His people when they stood before the temple in His presence (see 2 Chronicles 20:5-9). Jehoshaphat clearly had great confidence in the outcome, to be able to make a statement like this before the battle. Presumably this was based on a promise that had been made to Jehoshaphat's great great grandfather Solomon that, conditional on His people humbling themselves, praying, and repenting, God would answer prayer made in the temple (see 2 Chronicles 7:14-15). Today we do not have to go to the temple in Jerusalem to find the spirit of faith to believe in God's promises (see John

4:21-24).

Generational curses can also be lifted by fasting and prayer. Numbers 14:18 makes it clear that there are consequences of sin that affect future generations. Leviticus 26:40-42 gives clear direction in the Old Covenant that confession had to be made not only of that generation's sins but also of the previous generation's. Nehemiah 9:1-2 tells us that the Israelites confessed their sins and the sins of their fathers, but prior to this they fasted in sackcloth. Daniel likewise humbled himself and fasted before confessing the people's sins and the sins of the fathers in Daniel 9:3-16. Jeremiah 31:29-34, which talks of the New Covenant, makes it clear that the curse of the law is not passed to the children today in the New Covenant (see also Hebrews 8:7-13). This does not mean there will not be some consequences of the sins of the fathers that will still affect the children—but this is not a spiritual curse—if it is broken in Christ, who became the curse in our place.

Some other examples from the Word of God concerning times to fast include national emergencies, as in Esther 4:3, and to ward off God's judgment, as in Jonah 3:4-7, 2 Samuel 12:16, Joel 2:12-14, and 1 Kings 21:27-29. Additional examples include escaping imminent danger, as in Daniel 6:18-23, to gain understanding, as in Daniel 9:20-22, anointing for ministry, as in Acts 13:2-3 and Acts 14:23, healing, as in Psalm 35:11-14 and Isaiah 58:8, and mourning, as in 1 Samuel 31:13.

Jesus made it clear that if we have too little faith, our ministry will be hindered. He recommended prayer and fasting to develop the faith level necessary to overcome challenges (see Matthew 17:20-21). If adequate faith cannot be mustered through prayer alone, fasting is called for. Judges 20:15-17 talks of a battle between Benjamin and the rest of Israel, and the advantage seemingly was with Israel with four hundred thousand men compared with the tribe of Benjamin's twenty-six thousand. They inquired of God who should attack first and having been told Judah, they attacked (see Judges 20:18-22). There is no mention in these scriptures of a confirmation that they should attack at that time—only of who should go first. After losing twenty-two thousand men, Israel again asked counsel of the LORD. They were told to go up again, and Israel lost another eighteen thousand men (see Judges 20:23-25). Following this setback, they fasted until evening and sacrificed and finally received confirmation that that they should not only go up again but that God would deliver the tribe of Benjamin into their hand (see Judges 20:26-28).

Matthew 6:16-18 makes it clear that fasting of some kind is not an option and that when we fast, we should do it in secret. The Pharisees fasted twice a week but omitted the weightier matters of the law—justice, mercy, and faith (see Matthew 23:23).

Fasting makes us hungry in both the natural and the spiritual man. Fasting helps prayer because it brings the Spirit of God, which draws us (see Song of Solomon 1:3-4) and quickens us to seek Him (see Psalm 80:18).

In all cases, fasting should be discussed with a medical professional before a fast is started.

Day 7

CHILDLIKE FAITH

Luke 18:17 tells us that *"whoever does not receive the kingdom of God as a little child will by no means enter it."* Matthew 18:3-4 reveals that one of the traits of childlike character we must have to enter the kingdom is humility, because whoever humbles himself as a little child is the greatest in the kingdom of heaven. Psalm 131 echoes the theme of the humility of a child.

Does He not promise to pour out His Spirit on our descendants and His blessings on our offspring? (see Isaiah 44:3)

Peter reminds us to humble ourselves and submit to one another because God resists the proud, but gives grace to the humble (see 1 Peter 5:5-6).

We have seen that the major requirements for answered prayer are that we continually abide in

Him and that His Word abides in us. We have seen the importance of having faith in the promises of God and how that faith can increase as we access the kingdom and read the Word of God. Elijah talked of hearing the sound of abundance of rain before praying seven times until the evidence of a small cloud was seen (see 1 Kings 18:41-45). The prayer of Elijah for rain to produce the earth's fruit is given as an example of an effective, fervent prayer of a righteous man in James 5:16-18. The effects of the kingdom of God can be as imperceptible as a crop growing in the ground, but the harvest is sure even if we do not know how the faith grows (see Mark 4:26-29).

We have seen the importance of taking steps to protect our faith in the promises of God and avoid unbelief. We must walk by faith and not by sight. We know that some of the conditions necessary for access to the kingdom and being in Him include being poor in spirit, unity among believers, submission to God, praise and worship, thanksgiving, death to self and to sin, confession of sin, and of course, seeking first His kingdom and His righteousness.

The disciples were told by Jesus to stay in Jerusalem after His ascension until they were endued with power (see Luke 24:49). *"The kingdom of God is not in word but in power"* (1 Corinthians 4:20).

The subject that Jesus talked to His disciples about in the forty days between His resurrection and His ascension was the kingdom of God (see Acts 1:1-3).

When Jesus talked of baptizing them with the Holy Spirit, the disciples asked Him about the restoration of an earthly kingdom to Israel. Based on what they had already heard, they apparently linked the baptism with the Holy Spirit with the kingdom of God. Jesus made it clear that they would receive power after the Holy Spirit came upon them. The reason why they were endued with power was to be witnesses, firstly in Jerusalem, then ultimately to the ends of the earth (see Acts 1:4-8, Luke 24:45-49, Mark 16:20, John 15:16, and Revelation 12:11).

Paul stated that his preaching was *"not with persuasive words of human wisdom, but in demonstration of the Spirit and of power, that your faith should not be in the wisdom of men but in the power of God"* (1 Corinthians 2:4-5).

Should our teaching and preaching be any different?

Day 8

Intercessory Loop

A prayer model for intercession might look like
Figure 4 (see page 69). Remember, there are different levels of prayer and we are to use them all.
Paul tells us to pray with all prayer (literally, every order of praying) and supplication in the Spirit
(see Ephesians 6:18). God has wondered where
the intercessors are (see Ezekiel 22:30 and Isaiah
59:16). Intercession involves getting to the point
where the assurance is so great that all that re-
mains before the answer is manifested is thanksgiving and a protection from anything that might
damage that assurance. In this model it is specific
intercession that is being discussed, and not just
some general prayer.

There are only two possibilities as we start
intercession—either we believe God has answered (not just that God has the ability to answer) even if our eyes haven't yet seen the an-

swer, or we don't believe He has answered.

If we believe, then we have our answer to prayer and Mark 11:24 is fulfilled. We need to continue to abide in Him and have the Word in us to protect our faith until the answer is manifested (see John 15:7). If we are not yet assured of the answer, then we must increase our faith. We can do this by hearing the Word (see Romans 10:17). If this does not suffice, then we must not only continue to hear His Word but also move on in the model loop and also be sure we are truly *"in Him."* If we are truly in Him, then all we need to do is ask according to His will (see 1 John 5:14-15). Unfortunately, many read this verse as "If we ask anything according to His will," He hears us and grants our petition. They omit the *"in Him."* Likewise, those who claim God's promises and quote 2 Corinthians 1:20 also need to be *"in Him."* Perhaps fasting is called for to bring a greater presence of the Holy Spirit to combat any lingering unbelief.

As we have discussed in earlier chapters, the presence of the Spirit is necessary to be truly *"in Him,"* and He is the source of the faith we need (see Romans 8:26, 1 Timothy 1:14, and Acts 3:16).

We have to build up our faith, praying in the Spirit, according to Jude 20 and keep testing ourselves to see if Mark 11:24 is fulfilled. If it is not, then we need to go around the loop again and again until it is fulfilled and we have the assurance we need. When the disciples asked Jesus to increase their faith, the response was that all that was needed was a mustard seed of faith to start with (see Luke 17:4-5).

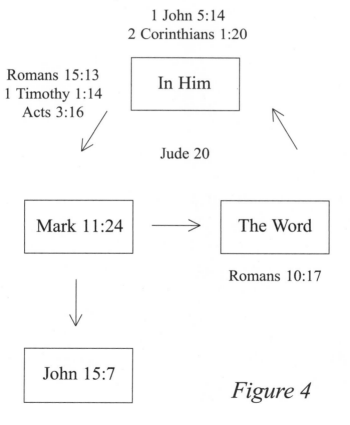

Figure 4

Intercession can be hard work. The main obstructions to answered prayer are often the same as the obstructions to being *"in Him."*

How can we be sure that we are fully *"in Him"*? We can only abide *"in Him"* if the anointing abides in us (see 1 John 2:27). According to 1 John 2:3-6, we know that we are *"in Him"* if the love of God has been perfected in us. We know that we are perfected in love if all fear has been removed from our lives and we are casting every care on Him, trusting Him in every situation where fear may arise (see 1 John 4:17-18). This is what He means by obeying His commandment to believe on (trust) the name of Jesus Christ. If we love one another, which is His second commandment in 1 John 3:23-24, then we remove basic obstructions to being fully *"in Him."*

Without an individual experiencing the power of trusting in God, there can be a barrier built up to protect that person from a repeat of painful past experiences which have made it difficult to trust again. This barrier is based on fear and manifests itself as insecurity and low self-esteem and can involve:

1. denial of the truth to protect the individual from painful shame-based feelings that they might be criticized for not knowing the truth (almost certainly based on life experiences of being criticized whenever a mistake has been made).

2. deflection of the truth by attacking, blaming, or accusing others to create an impression of superiority and control to offset the shame-based feelings (to feel better).

3. dependencies to provide a temporary cure for the pain of the shame-based feelings via drugs, alcohol, overwork, etc. Even religion based on works falls into the dependent category. Unfortunately, this results in a cycle where the consequence of dependency makes the person feel more internal pain and shame following the temporary high, so that they have to resort to the dependency to dull the pain again.

The barriers created to protect from shame can result in isolation, stubbornness, and denial and be a powerful resistance to accepting salvation and truly being *"in Him."* We must realize that the world will continue to turn if we completely lay down our lives for God and man and that all things work for good in Christ whether or not we can see the end result. This trust brings the supernatural peace that surpasses all understanding.

These obstructions to being *"in Him"* manifest not only as fear or the absence of self-sacrificing love, but also as such things as unconfessed sin, unforgiveness, disunity, failure to submit, spiritual oppression, prayerlessness, unthankfulness, and failure to give praise. Fasting will help reveal and remove obstructions as it brings the spirit of revelation. As we continue to go around the loop, obstacles will be removed, faith will be increased, and our breakthrough will come.

Though it is important to have faith enough to remove the mountains obstructing our lives, we are nothing without love (see 1 Corinthians 13:2). *"Greater love has no one than this, than to lay down one's life for his friends"* (John 15:13). We need to abide in His love (see John 15:9-12). We are promised that if we keep His commandment to love one another, we will abide in His love. In other words, if we die daily as Paul did, then that love is *"poured out into our hearts by the Holy Spirit"* (Romans 5:5).

This study has been looking at how to access the kingdom. Matthew 7:13-14 is a familiar part of Scripture taken traditionally as referring to eternal life, telling us to enter by the narrow gate and warning us that few find it. Reading the preceding verses 7 to12, the context is prayer in asking, seeking, and knocking.

Whether Matthew 7:14 is talking of spiritual life in this world, eternal life, or both, one thing is clear: We need to know Him. By this we know that we know Him, if we obey His commandments to believe (trust) in Him and love one another (see 1 John 2:3). There will come a day when many people will think they can enter the kingdom but cannot, despite doing great wonders (see Matthew 7:21-23). When Jesus says He NEVER knew them, it does not refer to backsliding. Knowing Jesus necessitates a demonstration of love for others, particularly the poor and needy (see Jeremiah 22:16 and Matthew 25:31-40).

We need to be led by the Spirit. If we try to do things with selfish motives devoid of love, it is worthless. If we fail to be filled with the Spirit and led by the Spirit, we will miss the mark.

It is interesting to read 1 John 2:12-14. The children—the new converts—know the Father because no one can even come to Christ unless the Father draws him (see John 6:44). It is through the Father's goodness that we are drawn to repentance so that our sins are forgiven (see Romans 2:4). The young men are those who are more mature—they have learned the art of spiritual warfare and have overcome the wicked one. They have become strong, and the Word of God abides in them. However, it is the fathers, who have fathered other converts already, who truly know Christ—Him who is from the beginning (see also 1 John 1:1). It is Christ who baptizes with the Spirit so that we can be endued with power to be His witnesses to the ends of the earth (see Mark 1:8, Acts 1:8, and Acts 2:33). It is also interesting to note the words of John the Baptist, who said he did not know Jesus despite being His relative (see John 1:32-33). As we have already discussed, he who was least in the kingdom was greater than John. Without knowing Christ, we cannot enter the kingdom.

Day 9

CONFRONTING SIN IN THE CAMP

When the disciples asked the Lord to increase their faith, He said that even if their faith was small, as a mustard seed, the basis was present to speak to the issue and it would be done. Their faith was necessary to find the answer to their prayer, and the disciples sought an increase in faith accordingly. Is it not our duty to use the servant we have been given, namely faith, to fulfill the will of God in our lives before taking rest from prayer? (see Luke 17:5-10) Is it not the work of God that we should *"believe in Him whom He sent"* (John 6:29)? It is not without significance that the two preceding verses talk of confronting our brother and forgiving him, in the context of increasing our faith in prayer (see Luke 17:3-4).

We have already seen that whatever things we

ask for in prayer, if we believe that we receive them, we shall have them (see Mark 11:22-24).

These verses also include the concept of having faith and speaking to the issue, of which more will be said later. A major key to successful prayer is again mentioned in the following verse, Mark 11:25—namely, forgiveness. If our minds are cluttered with unforgiveness and bitterness, it leaves less room for the Holy Spirit to increase our faith.

Matthew 18:15-20 gives clear instruction about how to confront our brother. It isn't enough to forgive our brother in the church if he continues in sin, as the Spirit is grieved and the faith of the body will suffer and prayer will be hindered. There has to be accountability and confrontation of sin in the church. One translation of verse 18 says: *"Whatever you bind on earth will be—having been bound in heaven and whatever you loose on earth will be—having been loosed in heaven."* The implication here is that in the realm of the kingdom of heaven the prayer is already answered—we just need to connect with the kingdom and the prayer will be answered on earth. This prayer is hindered if the proper protocols in confronting sin are not followed by confronting it yourself, with one or two friends, or ultimately with the church. The prayer of agreement is powerful, as it is in the presence of two or three witnesses that the truth of this is established (see verse 16) and the Lord is in their midst (see verse 20)—but only if sin is confronted. Connected with the confrontation of sin is forgiveness. The following verses again reinforce the importance of forgiveness, followed by a parable likening the kingdom of heaven to a king and his servants showing forgiveness. The consequence for not forgiving our brother is severe (see Matthew 18:21-35).

The story of Achan reinforces this principle of confronting sin in the camp. Because Achan had taken some of the accursed things, the children of Israel were unable to stand against the men of Ai. The LORD threatened to remove His presence unless the sin was dealt with (see Joshua 7:10-13). Complacency leads to drought until the Spirit is poured out from on high (see Isaiah 32:9-15). However, *"God is greatly to be feared in the assembly of the saints"* (Psalm 89:7). The story of Ananias and Sapphira illustrates the deadly judgments on those who *"lie to the the Holy Spirit"* (see Acts 5:1-11). An Old Testament example is Gehazi contracting leprosy when he was disobedient to Elisha and sought material things (see 2 Kings 5:26-27). *"The LORD will judge His people,"* and *"it is a fearful thing to fall into the hands of the living God"* if the Spirit of grace is insulted (see Hebrews 10:26-31). Paul demonstrates the power available to the church to confront sin in the church when the power of the Lord Jesus Christ is present (see 1 Corinthians 3-6). It is not without significance that *"the Spirit of the LORD"* is referred to as *"the Spirit of knowledge AND of the fear of the LORD"* (Isaiah 11:2).

We have seen that seeking first the kingdom is necessary to bring the presence of God into our prayer life. In Psalm 141 David is crying out to God to hear his prayer and asking that any hindrances to prayer through anything he might say or do be removed. The rebuke of a righteous man brings oil upon the head in Psalm 141:5. Is this not a reference to the presence of the Holy Spirit, which facilitates faith in prayer?

In our dealings with the world and the evil person, we are required to turn the other cheek (see

Matthew 5:39). This is not the case among believers—sin must be confronted. To believe in Him means to trust in Him—if we have this abiding trust in all situations, we can let down our defenses and love one another as commanded. Romans 13:8-14 states that *"love is the fulfillment of the law,"* and that we are to *"put on the Lord Jesus Christ, and make no provision for the flesh, to fulfill its lusts."* We put on Christ when we are baptized into Christ, when we are baptized into His death (see Romans 6:3 and Galatians 3:27).

Faith requires actions and humility. Great warnings were given against spiritual pride, for example, in Luke 10:17-20, where Jesus' disciples were told not to rejoice in the fact that demonic spirits were subject to them. Paul was told to stop praying about his thorn in the flesh, which had been given lest he *"be exalted above measure"* (2 Corinthians 12:7-9). God's strength is made perfect in weakness—it is better to forgo pride and have the power of Christ resting upon us.

The Word declares that it has been granted to us *"on behalf of Christ, not only to believe in Him, but also to suffer for His sake"* (Philippians 1:29).

When we are persecuted for righteousness' sake, we receive the kingdom of heaven (see Matthew 5:10). When we are brought before authorities for Jesus' sake, we have abundant access to the kingdom of heaven and it is the Holy Spirit Himself who will speak on our behalf (see Mark 13:11).

In Romans 8:16-18, when *"the Spirit Himself bears witness with our spirit that we are children of God,"* the context again is suffering, and Paul states that the glory of God far outweighs the sufferings. Peter tells us not to be concerned about our trials because if we are reproached for the name of Christ, the Spirit of glory and of God rests on us (see 1 Peter 4:12-14).

Tribulation brings forth perseverance and, ultimately the Holy Spirit (see Romans 5:3-5). In the familiar Psalm 23, the anointing oil of the Holy Spirit is present when David is in the presence of his enemies. Psalm 92:8-11 again illustrates the principle that not only are God's people pursued by enemies, but also that when they are pursued, they are anointed by fresh oil of the Holy Spirit. There is something wrong if God's people fail to encounter resistance.

Day 10

I BELIEVED,
THEREFORE I SPOKE

The Book of Proverbs confirms the power of
the spoken word:

*There is one who speaks like the piercings of
a sword, but the tongue of the wise promotes
health.* Proverbs 12:18

*Anxiety in the heart of man causes depres-
sion, but a good word makes it glad.*
Proverbs 12:25

*Pleasant words are like a honeycomb,
sweetness to the soul and health to the bones.*
Proverbs 16:24

Death and life are in the power of the tongue,
and those who love it will eat its fruit.
Proverbs 18:21

It is out of the abundance of the heart that the mouth speaks (see Matthew 12:34 and Luke 6:45). If the heart of a man is not right with God, it will be revealed—by their fruits you shall know them. Our words are supposed to impart grace to the hearers (see Ephesians 4:29).

The Aaronic benediction spoken by the priests over the children of Israel in Numbers 6:22-27 again consists of spoken words. *"The LORD bless you and keep you; the LORD make His face shine upon you, and be gracious to you; the LORD lift up His countenance upon you, and give you peace."* According to the Word of God, the purpose for speaking these words was to put His name on the children of Israel and bless them.

What does putting His name on the people mean? Exodus 33:15-23 tells us that when Moses asked to see God's glory, the LORD said He would make all His goodness pass before him and proclaim the name of the LORD before him. The name of the LORD is a manifestation of the very character of God in all His goodness and graciousness and compassion. The glory of God is the presence of God. When the love of God is poured out in our hearts by the Holy Spirit, then the very character of God should be manifested in our lives and in what we say. When the priests spoke the blessing, there was spiritual power in the words which put the presence of God on the people so that the character of God might be manifested in their lives.

When we end a prayer with the words "in Jesus' name," it is not some magical incantation that will result in our prayer being answered. When Jesus said, *"If you ask anything in My name,"* in John 14:13-14, surely the idea was to be filled with the Spirit as we prayed (seek first His kingdom and His righteousness) so that the presence of God and the character of God would be involved in the prayer. Unless we are *"in Him,"* we cannot pray in His name. The name of the Lord Jesus needs to be glorified in us and we *"in Him"* (see 2 Thessalonians 1:11-12). We have talked much in the preceding chapters about being *"in Him."*

The purpose of the Aaronic priesthood was to

minister to the LORD and bless in His name (see
Deuteronomy 21:5). According to Peter, we are
*"a chosen generation, a royal priesthood, a holy
nation"* (1 Peter 2:9). In the book of Revelation,
John says we have been made kings and priests
(see Revelation 1:4-6). If the purpose of a priest
is to bring the presence of God on the people by
blessing in His name, then it is clear that part of
our job description is to bring the presence of God
into the world. We will speak more of this at a
later time, but for now let us continue to discuss
the power of the anointed spoken word.

There is divine power in the spoken word of
blessing. Genesis 24:60 records the blessing spoken by Rebekah's family before she departed to
become Isaac's wife. They said, *"May you become the mother of thousands of ten thousands."*
Her younger son, Jacob, fathered the twelve tribes
of Israel. Consequently, Rebekah fulfilled the
blessing.

The story of Isaac blessing his sons is well
known, but what is often overlooked is that this
blessing was to be done *"in the presence of the
LORD"* (Genesis 27:5-7).

The blessing of Jacob by Isaac is given in Genesis 27:27-29. Even though Jacob received the blessing of his father through deceit, this could not be changed so that the older son, Esau, could receive the blessing instead (see Genesis 27:36-40). The words of the blessing were spoken in the presence of the LORD and were irrevocable.

Moses was told to take his rod and speak to the rock in Numbers 20:8. When Moses struck the rock instead, he was rebuked because he did not believe the LORD (see verse 12). When the disciples asked Jesus to increase their faith, He told them to speak to the mulberry tree in Luke 17:5-6. In response to Peter talking about the withered fig tree, Jesus said they should have faith in God and speak to the mountain in Mark 11:20-23.

There is incredible power available in the word spoken under the anointing of the Holy Spirit. *"You will also declare a thing, and it will be established for you"* (Job 22:28). *"He who supplies the Spirit to you and works miracles among you"* does it *"by the HEARING of faith"* (Galatians 3:5). In the New Testament the word was spoken in the name of the LORD—in other words, in the presence of God under the anointing—with boldness to bring about healing, as in Acts 3:6. There were no recorded instances of people praying, "Lord, heal so and so," as they had already sought the Healer, not the healing. They spoke in faith with the *"spirit of faith"* (2 Corinthians 4:13). To act in faith, they protected that faith by removing any chance of unbelief, they prayed to receive the source of that spirit of faith, and then they spoke to the issue, as in Acts 9:40. If the words of the blessing spoken by Isaac under conditions of deceit were irrevocable, how much more should our blessings and prayers of faith be anointed to take effect in the name of Jesus Christ of Nazareth.

May the Lord bless you and may you prosper in all things and be in health (see 3 John 2).

Day 11

DAILY BREAD
AND CUP

Wisdom invites those who lack understanding: *"Come, eat of my bread and drink of the wine I have mixed"* (Proverbs 9:5). It is probably not without significance that the feeding of the five thousand took place near the time of the Passover and preceded a discourse on flesh and blood and the importance of our being in Him, and He in us (see John 6:4).

Jesus made it clear that we need to labor for the food that endures to eternal life and that He will give us food if we do the work of God—namely, to believe, to trust in Him (see John 6:27-29). It is clear that this food is His flesh, and is the Bread of Life (see John 6:48-51).

The importance of abiding in Him has been discussed at length. Jesus stated that whoever eats His flesh and drinks His blood abides in Him. They will have eternal life and Jesus will raise them up at the last day (see John 6:54-56). A few verses later, in John 6:63, Jesus makes it clear that it is the Spirit who gives life and that the flesh profits nothing. Believing (trusting) in Him, by dying to ourselves and our fears, makes room for the infilling of the Spirit.

It is therefore extremely important to grasp what it means to believe. To believe on the Lord means essentially to trust in the Lord. John 3:16 tells us that *"whoever* believes *in Him should not perish but have everlasting life."* This is not just a belief in the existence of Jesus Christ or in something He said, but rather an implicit trust in Him in all things regardless of the consequences. *"As many as received Him, to them He gave the right to become children of God, to those who* believe *in His name"* (John 1:12). He who *believes* has everlasting life, but the wrath of God abides on those who do not believe (see John 3:18 and 3:36).

Believing on the Lord Jesus Christ leads to baptism in the name of the Lord Jesus and baptism of the Holy Spirit with preaching of the kingdom of God (see Acts 19:4-8). Whoever *believes* in Jesus, as the Scripture has said, will have rivers of living water flowing out of his heart. When Jesus said this, He was referring to the giving of the Holy Spirit, which could only happen after He was glorified (see John 7:38-39). In Acts 11:16-17, Peter is talking of the baptism of the Holy Spirit which he says they received when they *believed* on the Lord Jesus Christ. Jesus said that those who *believed* in Him would do *"greater works"* (John 14:12).

The Spirit of Christ given by the Father will abide with us forever and teaches us ALL things and brings to remembrance ALL things taught by Jesus (see John 14:16-18 and 26). It is God who establishes us in Christ and seals us and gives us the Spirit as a guarantee (see 2 Corinthians 1:21-22). It is Jesus who baptizes with the Holy Spirit (see John 1:29-34 and Act 2:33). His disciples were commanded to remain in Jerusalem until they received power to become witnesses (see Acts 1:4-8). The Helper sent by Jesus *"will convict the world of sin, and of righteousness, and of judgment"* (see John 16:7-8). Jesus is to be glorified in us (see John 17:10).

The second part of communion is to drink of His blood. His blood is the wine of communion which removes our sins and brings healing, but it does require that we confess our sins. If we confess our sins to one another and pray for one another, we shall be healed (see James 5:16). When Hezekiah reinstated the Passover, the blood of lambs that covered sin brought healing to people who had not even sanctified themselves (see 2 Chronicles 30:15-20). How much more should the blood of the Lamb of God remove sin and heal. There is salvation and healing at the cross (see 1 Peter 2:21-24).

The heart of the Lord's Prayer refers to this communion of daily bread and forgiveness of sin (see Luke 11:1-4).The purpose of prayer is to petition, *"Your kingdom come, Your will be done, on earth as it is in heaven,"* and to establish the rule of heaven on earth. Our daily bread is to believe and trust in Christ and die to ourselves, in order that the true Bread of Heaven, Jesus Christ, may have a place in our lives. Is not the request in the Lord's Prayer *"Give us day by day our daily bread"* a reference to the bread of communion sacrifice? Also, is not the cup of wine representative of the blood of Jesus that takes away the sin of the world? And when we pray, *"Forgive us our sins,"* are we not partakers of the communion wine? A key element of forgiveness is forgiving others, and is this not also stated in the Lord's Prayer, *"Forgive us our sins, for we also forgive"* ?

The introduction to First Peter talks of the elect being in *"sanctification of the Spirit for obedience and sprinkling of the blood of Jesus Christ"* (1 Peter 1:2). Does this not imply the elect eating His flesh and drinking His blood?

We need self-examination before communion and we need DAILY bread. Daily communion creates a relationship that daily removes all concern about earthly values and the need to complain or covet or lust, and likewise provides a daily reminder of the critical importance of death to sin, self, and fear, in order that we may truly abide "in Him."

We are exhorted as a body of believers to *"consider one another in order to stir up love and good works, not forsaking the assembling of ourselves together"* (Hebrews 10:24-25). It is the partaking of the flesh and blood of Christ that allows our access to the heavenly Holy of Holies and to be truly abiding in Him and He in us (see Hebrews 10:19-23 and John 6:56). As Spirit-filled temples we can then act as effective conduits to encourage and impart spiritual strength to our brothers and sisters in Christ.

Day 12

SALT OF THE EARTH

Isaiah 43:7 says that every one of God's people has been created for the glory of God. Is this not to bear the glory of God in the world and flavor the world as the salt of the earth? We are called *"for the obtaining of the glory of our Lord Jesus Christ"* (2 Thessalonians 2:14). Christ needs to be formed in us for the Father to draw people to His Son (see John 6:44).

After talking of the kingdom belonging to the poor in spirit and the persecuted in the Sermon on the Mount, Jesus tells His disciples that they are the salt of the earth and that the salt must keep its flavor or the world will not be seasoned (see Matthew 5:13). Does not the salt refer to the presence of the Holy Spirit? In Mark 9:49-50, Jesus says that every sacrifice will be seasoned with salt and that we should have salt in ourselves.

The anointing is so critical. We cannot save our-selves—we can only be drawn by the Spirit to Jesus Christ. If the anointed believer is only present today, it would be wise for the unbeliever to receive salvation today—as the Spirit-filled be-liever may not be present tomorrow and the op-portunity may be lost. Psalm 85:9 says, *"Surely His salvation is near to those who fear Him, that glory may dwell in our land."* The purpose of be-ing anointed is to bring the unbeliever into closer contact with the Spirit of God. Because God loves righteousness and hates wickedness, the anoint-ing was sent into the world to change it (see Psalm 45:6-7 and Hebrews 1:8-9). Does not Psalm 67 call for the presence of God on His people—that He may cause His face to shine on us, that God's ways may be known on earth and His salvation among all nations?

In John 17:22-24 it is clear that the reason we are in Him and have received His glory is so that the world may know that Jesus Christ has been sent. The condition necessary for people to know that God's people are His disciples is that God's people love one another (see John 13:34-35). When we love one another, laying down our lives

for one another, we make room for the Spirit, and
it is the Spirit who brings revelation to the world.

In 2 Chronicles 7:14, the promise to His people
is that if they will humble themselves and pray,
He will heal their land. When God's people repent, the Spirit rests upon them to bring God's
presence into the world to change it for the better.
Hypocrisy must be eliminated among God's
people or the world will not be seasoned with salt.
When the leaven of hypocrisy was present, not
only were there fewer people fed and fewer left-
overs, but also Jesus left the people and got into
the boat immediately with His disciples after feeding the four thousand (see Mark 8:9-10). After
feeding the five thousand, Jesus sent His disciples
away and stayed with the people before sending
them away (see Mark 6:45). John's version in-
cludes the detail that the feeding of the five thousand occurred near the time of the Passover Feast
(see John 6:4). Therefore, it would have had great
significance for His audience who would have
been purging leaven out of their homes. Leaven
will spread through dough if it is present—it must
be eliminated (see Exodus 13:7). If the fish are
symbolic of the people feeding the crowds, then

we need to purge out the leaven and become the two fish in agreement to feed the five thousand, not the few small fish recorded as feeding the four thousand. If the Passover is a foreshadowing of our partaking of Jesus Christ's flesh and blood—the bread and the cup—then we need to purge ourselves of the leaven by examining ourselves and not eat in an unworthy manner (see 1 Corinthians 11:27-32).

Day 13

REPAIRER OF
THE BREACH

The story of Nehemiah provides a good illustration of the resistance that can be expected when we set out to rebuild the waste places and repair the breach spoken of in Isaiah 58:12, which is a promise from God if we fast with the fast He has chosen. Following fasting, confession, and repentance for generational sin, Nehemiah took up the challenge and went to Jerusalem with a vision to rebuild the wall and the gates in Nehemiah 1:4-6.

First of all, the local people, namely Sanballat and Tobiah, were deeply disturbed that someone should seek the well-being of the children of Israel (see Nehemiah 2:10). They laughed at Nehemiah and despised him when he suggested rebuilding the walls (see verses 17-19). They became furious and very indignant, and mocked the Jews when they heard the work had started (see Nehemiah 4:1-3). They became angry and conspired to attack them and cause confusion when they heard that the gaps were being filled (see verses 7-8). Can we expect any less as we stand in the gap? (see Ezekiel 22:30)

There will be resistance to any work of restoration. There will be a need to keep watch and be armed, as the enemy will plan to attack (see Nehemiah 4:11). There will be a need to eliminate oppression among God's people and restore lands and crops and houses (see Nehemiah 5:10-11). The enemy will try repeatedly to distract from the task at hand and do harm (see Nehemiah 6:2-4). They will threaten and try to create fear (see verses 5-9). They will hire people to bring fear and try to find a cause for an evil report (see Nehemiah 6:10-13). False prophets will try to provoke fear (see verse 14). The enemy will try to infiltrate—in Nehemiah's case by intermarriage—causing pledges to be made (see verse 18).

There was a need for spiritual revival. It was important to reinstate the reading of the Law, which was done on the first day of the seventh month and following the instruction in the Law (see Nehemiah 7:73-8:3). It was important to re-instate the Feast of Tabernacles, which had not been observed since Joshua's time (see Nehemiah 8:17). It was important for the people to confess their sins and separate themselves from the people of the land. The infiltration had even included moving into the house of God and the replace-ment of tithes of grain, new wine, oil, and frank-incense with Tobiah's belongings when Nehemiah was absent (see Nehemiah 13:4-9). We need to be on our guard, as the same strategies will be employed by our enemies to discourage and try to destroy us if we decide to rebuild the waste places.

On the subject of restoration, the call of Gideon is also worthy of study. He asked for a sign and after he made an offering, a sign was given and Gideon found peace (see Judges 6). His **first** ac-tion was to destroy idolatry despite fear of the men of the city and of his own household (see verses 25-27). Enemies came against him, but the Spirit of the LORD came upon Gideon—the literal Hebrew says that the Lord clothed Himself with Gideon (see verse 34). How much more should we be temples of the Holy Spirit. Gideon acted in faith, calling the tribes *before* he asked for two more signs (see verses 34-40). Is it not that he had faith that he wanted to keep rather than unbelief that made him ask for the signs of the dew on the fleece and on the ground? Does not the dew speak of the Spirit? (see Psalm 133) Gideon selected the three hundred who were on their feet ready for action like the three thousand on the Day of Pentecost (see Judges 7:7). Again, he received a sign with the enemy's dream of the barley bread and its interpretation. His men blew trumpets and broke pitchers to reveal light, just as we must be broken to reveal light. His enemies were made to turn against each other (see Judges 7:9-22 and Psalm 83:9-18).

Day 14

WELLS OF
OUR FATHERS

Isaiah 49:8-9 tells that the Messiah will be given as a covenant to the people to restore the earth and cause them to inherit desolate heritages.

Related to the previous subject of rebuilding the waste places, we have seen that this restoration is facilitated by a fast because it brings the presence of the Holy Spirit to break the yoke of bondage.

Abram after returning from Egypt went back to the place where he had first built an altar to the LORD between Bethel and Ai and called on the name of the LORD (see Genesis 13:1-4). When Jacob first went to Bethel, he poured out oil on the stone. When he returned the second time, he poured out a drink offering (wine) and oil (see

Genesis 28:18 and 35:14). Did not these men return to the places where they had experienced the
presence of God before, knowing that they might
experience Him there again?

It is interesting to note that Jacob went back to
Beersheba before going to Egypt. There was a
spiritual well in Beersheba that he had experienced
before, and he went there again to see a vision
(see Genesis 46:1-2). When Abraham died, the
Philistines stopped up the wells of water that he
had dug. The Philistines were an envious people,
and when they told Isaac to leave their territory,
Isaac dug again the wells of his father (see Genesis 26:12-18). In a spiritual sense, do we not need
to return to those places and conditions where the
presence of God was manifested?

Samuel traveled to the three cities of Mizpah,
Gilgal, and Bethel every year (see 1 Samuel 7:16).
These three cities are worthy of study. At *Mizpah*,
which means "watchtower", the people humbled
themselves after putting away their idols and then
fasted and sacrificed. Water was poured out there
before the LORD which reminds us of the Feast of
Tabernacles (see 1 Samuel 7:4-11). Their enemies

were defeated. It was also at a town called Mizpah that Jephthah was raised up, after the children of Israel had put away their idols (see Judges 10:16-18). Again their enemies were defeated when the Spirit of the LORD came upon Jephthah and he advanced toward the people of Ammon from Mizpah of Gilead (see Judges 11:29-30).

At Gilgal on the plains of Jericho, the reproach of Egypt was rolled away and the Passover was kept when Joshua first arrived in the Promised Land (see Joshua 5:9-11). It was from here that Joshua encountered the Commander of the Lord's army on the holy ground by Jericho (see verses 13-15). At Bethel, Jacob encountered the house of God and the gate of heaven where God spoke with him (see Genesis 28:16-19). The spiritual warfare in such a place must be maintained, as it is a breeding ground for idolatry. Jacob ordered the removal of all idols at his return in Genesis 35:1-15 and spoke with God, but this eventually became the place of Jeroboam's golden calf (see 1 Kings 12:28-29).

It is also of note that it was in some of these same locations—namely Gilgal, Bethel, and Jericho—that Elijah tested Elisha before he departed in the fiery chariot (see 2 Kings 2:1-4). Just as we must guard against the return of evil spirits in places where the Spirit has been poured out, we must guard our bodies, the temple of the Holy Spirit, and not allow ourselves to become complacent, for just as surely as an evil spirit will attack a place of former glory, he will also seek out the man whose house is swept and put in order and bring with him seven spirits more wicked than himself to dwell there (see Matthew 12:43-45 and Luke 11:24-26).

Day 15

MOUNTAINS
AND HILLS

The mountains are where the shepherds need to be, as this speaks of more intimacy with God and a greater fervency in prayer. When the shepherds go from mountain to hill, they lead the children of God astray and they become lost sheep. Their resting place needs to be on the mountain, separate from the world (see Jeremiah 50:6).

Matthew 5:1-12 states that Jesus was *seated* on a mountain when He taught His disciples that the poor in spirit and the persecuted are blessed and receive the kingdom. In Luke 6:12-23, He had been on a mountain all night in prayer, and when He had come down, He *stood* on a level place and taught the people who had come to hear Him and be healed. Power went out from Him to heal all the people. To be able to minister with effect on the plain where the world is, we need to have spent some time learning from the Master on the mountain and having our faith increased in the presence of the Master.

There is an interesting progression of events in the life of David that bears some resemblance to our own struggles. When Saul was persecuting David every day, David stayed in the strongholds and remained in the mountains in the Wilderness of Ziph (see 1 Samuel 23:14). *Ziph* means "falsehood" and speaks of the world. When the Ziphites went to Saul and told him of David's whereabouts, David was no longer in the mountains, but in the hill of Hachilah (see verse 19). *Hachilah* means "hope" and suggests that David, having built up His faith on the mountain, now had enough faith to descend to the hill of hope (faith is the substance of things hoped for) but was not quite ready to face the world. However, by the time the Ziphites had returned to Ziph before Saul, David and his men had moved to the Wilderness of Maon in the plain. *Maon* means "sin" and most certainly speaks of the world (see verse 24). Evidently David's faith had been increased over time, especially in view of the fact that Jonathan encouraged David between the mountain of truth and the hill of hope. David had to remove himself from the world and its sin to get his faith increased on the mountain. When his faith had been increased to a high level, he could maintain his faith in the plain of the wilderness of sin. When Saul pursued him there, he found the rock, where he could take refuge until Saul was distracted by the Philistines and left (see 1 Samuel 23:25-29). It is interesting to note that David eventually found himself in the Wilderness of Paran after sparing Saul's life in the cave. *Paran* means "glory" (see 1 Samuel 25:1).

There is a progression from mountains to hills that produces a depth with God. This can be seen in Psalm 42:6-7: Going from the heights of Hermon to the Hill Mizar results in deep calling to deep, speaking of an intimate relationship with God. This parallels David's encounters with Saul in the wilderness. A study of the Hebrew roots of these words is interesting, as *Hermon* can be related to consecration and *Mizar* can be related to being brought low, as in being humbled. The dew of Hermon brought about by unity is likened to the anointing oil on the priest and speaks of the

Holy Spirit (see Psalm 133:1-3). We need to grow our faith on the mountaintop and protect ourselves from unbelief. Increasingly, we can come down from the mountain to the hills where there are more distractions to our faith and find that our trust in God is so great that we don't care what position we are in, as we know all things work together for good. This childlike humility leads to a deepening of our relationship with God. Again paralleling the story of David in the Wilderness of Maon, the psalmist speaks to God his Rock in the presence of his enemies (see Psalm 42:9).

Day 16

CALLED AND CHOSEN

Matthew 4:18-22 and Mark 1:16-20 talk of the first call of Simon Peter and Andrew, who were casting a net into the sea, and of James and John, who were mending their nets in the boat. Jesus said, *"I WILL make you fishers of men."* Luke 5:1-10 tells of a separate occasion when Jesus saw two empty boats and the fishermen had gone to wash their nets. When they were called the second time, they were chosen and their boats were empty. Jesus entered Simon's boat to teach and told Simon to launch out into the deep, and Simon obeyed. When he caught many fish, he was convicted of his sinful nature and Jesus said, *"FROM NOW ON you will catch men."* Our earthly vessels also need to be empty of the things of the world if we are to make room for the Master to convict us of sin and to teach through us. We must also take that step of faith and launch out. Faith without works is dead. Evidently there was a period of growth between their first **call** to become fishers of men and being **chosen** for an immediate catch and the start of their ministry to catch men. According to John 15:2, every branch that bears fruit will be pruned so that it may bear more fruit. Why then should we be surprised when we go through periods of time when opportunities to produce fruit seem to be out of reach?

We are apparently not chosen immediately for service, like Joseph, who languished in a prison with his gift of interpretation inspite of having ruled Potiphar's house. Until the time that His word came to pass, the word of the LORD tested him (see Psalm 105:17-22). After the test, Joseph was chosen to have power to rule and bind princes. One thing Joseph probably had to deal with was forgiving his brothers for selling him into slavery.

Elisha is another Old Testament example of someone who was called and chosen. Elijah's mantle was first placed on Elisha when he was called to become his servant (see 1 Kings 19:19-21). It was not until Elisha had been tested in his persistence that he was chosen to receive the second mantle—the double portion of the spirit of Elijah—and begin his own miracle ministry after Elijah departed in the fiery chariot (see 2 Kings 2:9-15).

Clearly, those believing on the Lord are *"the called of Jesus Christ"* and *"called to be saints"* (Romans 1:6-7). Those who are with the Lord in the final battle with the ten kings and the beast are *"CALLED, CHOSEN, and faithful"* (Revelation 17:14). In the parable of the laborers in the vineyard, those who had worked all day and expected a greater reward than those who had worked a short time failed to understand that they were privileged to work in the vineyard and that many are called but few are chosen (see Matthew 20:1-16). This parable of the kingdom of heaven teaches us that the order or magnitude of rewards as we perceive them with worldly eyes is of little consequence.

Another parable likened the kingdom of heaven to a certain king who arranged a marriage feast for his son. After those who were initially called, namely Israel, declined the invitation, being more concerned with worldly issues, both the good and the bad out in the highways, namely the Gentiles, were gathered together to the wedding hall. (The invitation to the bad in this case is not based on past performance. They have the opportunity to repent and be saved, whereas the bad in the parable of the dragnet in Matthew 13:47-50 suffer an altogether different fate at the judgment at the end of the age.) The one without the wedding garment was cast into the outer darkness in the parable in Matthew 22:1-14. The wedding garments are fine linen, the righteous acts of the saints, according to Revelation 19:7-9. This parable concludes with Jesus saying again, *"Many are called, but few are chosen."* In this context, who are the called and who are the chosen? Does this imply that the one without the wedding garment was like the one who buried his talent, someone gifted and called to a ministry, but failing to bear fruit? We can only bear fruit if we abide in the vine as Jesus said in John 15:5. Evidently both of these men suffered the same fate in outer darkness (see Matthew 25:24-30).

According to Jude 11-19, people who knew the glory and yet rebelled, like Balaam, Korah, and

Cain, are in the blackness of darkness forever. End-time mockers of this type were prophesied. They attend the feasts of the church, but do not have the Spirit. The spirit of antichrist is on those who went out from the church not having the anointing of the Holy One (see 1 John 2:18-20), which implies that the antichrists are without the Spirit also.

They are of the world and speak as of the world, and the world hears them (see 1 John 4:5). When these deceivers and the spirit of antichrist that controls them do not confess Jesus as coming in the flesh (see 2 John 7 and 1 John 4:1-4), we remember the words of Jesus when He said that those who ate His flesh and drank His blood would abide in Him and He in them (see John 6:56) and that it isn't the flesh but the Spirit that gives life (see John 6:63).

Paul also talks of these people who in the latter times will depart from the faith, having a form of godliness but denying its power (see 1 Timothy 4:1-2 and 2 Timothy 3:1-5). When they do not confess Jesus as coming in the flesh, could it be that it is not so much the virgin birth of Jesus that they deny, but the eating of the "flesh" of Christ? Are not these the wolves in sheep's clothing who produce worldly fruit, having failed to enter by the narrow gate, and lead many astray? (see Matthew 7:13-20)

THE NARROW GATE

In Matthew 7:7-14 the instruction to enter by the narrow gate follows instruction on persisting in prayer. Just as few are chosen in the preceding discussion about the called and the chosen, there are few who find the way which leads to life because the gate is narrow and the way is difficult. The promise of the Father is to give good things, namely the Holy Spirit (see Luke 11:13).

After Jesus likens the kingdom of God to leaven hidden in meal, someone asks the question, *"Lord, are there few who are saved?"* Jesus says we need to know Him by entering the narrow gate; otherwise, when the door of the house is shut, we cannot enter (see Luke 13:20-27). In Luke's passage a distinction is made between the gate and the door of a house. John 10:9 tells us that we need to enter by the door of the sheepfold and go in and out and find pasture that we might be saved. Unless we know Him, and enter by the door of the sheepfold, we will practice lawlessness despite being in His presence and cannot enter the door of the kingdom of God. This passage in Luke finishes with the same words as the parable of the vineyard in Matthew 20:1-16—that there are those who are last who will be first and those who are first who will be last—where Jesus also said that many are called but few are chosen.

Following the warning to find life using the narrow gate, Matthew 7:15-20 warns of wolves in sheep's clothing discussed yesterday. Matthew 7:21-23 expands on this with the people crying out, *"Lord, Lord."* Despite having done signs and wonders, they are excluded because they do not know Jesus and consequently cannot do the will of the Father. The very next verses (24-27) remind us that it is of no value to have knowledge by hearing the Word and not apply it, or else the house will have no foundation and the storm will destroy it. Psalm 68:17-18 states that He gives gifts even to the rebellious that He might be there. The use of the word *Adonai* points to Christ and is confirmed by Ephesians 4:7-8 that this is a prophecy concerning Christ and the spreading of the kingdom power and presence of the Holy Spirit through rebellious men.

Matthew 8:10-13 talks of Abraham and Isaac and Jacob sitting in the kingdom, but the sons of the kingdom being cast into outer darkness, referring to the lack of faith in Israel. After Matthew's version of the parable of the leaven hidden in meal, the explanation of the parable of the tares is given in Matthew 13:36-43 and makes it clear that the sons of the kingdom are the good seed sown by the Son of Man. Jesus is clearly referring to the kingdom of heaven in both passages, so evidently the good seed sown by the Son of Man can find itself in outer darkness. Our instruction is to believe on Him and love one another. Paul tried to show us a more excellent way by pointing out that even if we have the faith to move mountains, if we don't have love, we are nothing and it profits us nothing (see 1 Corinthians 13:1-12).

The church of Philadelphia has an open door and the lukewarm church of Laodicea has a closed door—until they open it (see Revelation 3:8 and 3:20). A lukewarm church has no guarantee of white garments (see Revelation 3:18). It is only His sheep that hear His voice. And when we hear that voice, we need to dine with Him—eating of His flesh and drinking of His blood (see John 6:53-58). We need to be like the wise virgins who had oil in their vessels with their lamps, prepared for the wedding feast, or the door of the house will be shut (see Matthew 25:1-13).

Day 18

JUDGMENT

It is appointed for men once to die and then to be judged (see Hebrews 9:27). Paul, knowing the terror of the Lord, said, *"We must all appear before the judgment seat of Christ, that each one may receive the things done in the body, according to what he has done, whether good or bad"* (2 Corinthians 5:10-11). Elsewhere he said we should work out our salvation with fear and trembling (see Philippians 2:12-13). Judgment was a serious matter to Paul and we take it all too lightly in today's world. Peter obviously felt that it was a priority to mention that he was commanded to testify of the judgment of the living and the dead in his encounter with Cornelius (see Acts 10:42).

In Matthew 24:3 the disciples have two questions when they ask, *"What will be the sign of Your coming, and of the end of the age?"* In the rest of chapter 24 and in chapter 25 Jesus answers these questions in turn.

To those who eagerly wait for Him, Jesus will appear a second time (see Hebrews 9:28). The signs preceding His return are laid out, and His coming in great glory and the rapture are clearly indicated in Matthew 24:4-44. A very vivid picture is given in Luke 17:29-37, with fire and brimstone accompanying the return of the Son of Man. Those who have come to know the powers of the age to come, having freely received of the gifts of the Spirit (see Hebrews 6:4-5), are expected to produce fruit. The kingdom of heaven at His return is likened to five wise and five foolish virgins awaiting the arrival of the bridegroom. Only the anointed ones with the oil will be allowed in to the wedding (see Matthew 25:1-13).

The rewards to be given out at Jesus' return are laid out in the parable of the talents. Those who waste the opportunity to produce fruit are said to find themselves in the outer darkness, not in the eternal fire (see Matthew 25:14-30). Those who do not know God and those who do not obey the gospel will be punished with everlasting destruction from the presence of the Lord and from the glory of His power at His coming (see 2 Thessalonians 1:6-10).

Matthew 25:31-46 answers the second question about the end of the age and moves on from the coming of the Son of Man to talk of His being seated on the throne of His glory (see verse 31), followed by the judgment of the nations at the end of the age. At this judgment the sheep, who have done good to His brethren, are considered righteous and are allowed to inherit the kingdom. The goats are cast into the everlasting fire prepared for the devil and his angels.

The explanation of the parable of the wheat and tares, given in Matthew 13:24-30, makes it clear that the end of the age refers to the casting of the unrighteous into the fire, but the righteous into the kingdom of their Father. It is out of the kingdom of the Son that these are gathered, and only the righteous will shine forth in the kingdom of the Father (see Matthew 13:37-43). Is this not the end, when Jesus delivers the kingdom to God the Father? (see 1 Corinthians 15:24)

In Matthew 13:44-46, the kingdom of heaven is also likened to treasure hidden in a field and to a pearl of great price. This illustrates the value of the kingdom when people are prepared to sell everything to buy the priceless item. However, the kingdom of heaven is also likened to a dragnet in the sea gathering good and bad together at the end of the age (see Matthew 13:47-50). Does this not correspond to the sheep and goats judgment at the end of the age, leading the wicked to the everlasting fire prepared for the devil and his angels? (see Matthew 25:31-46)

In Daniel 12:2-3, talking of a time of Israel's deliverance, Daniel states that many of those sleeping in the dust of the earth will be raised, some to everlasting life and some to shame and everlasting contempt. As those who are wise will shine like the brightness of the firmament, and those who turn many to righteousness are like the stars forever and ever, is he not making reference to the judgment at Christ's return?

Revelation chapter 20 speaks of two judgments. First of all there is a judgment involving multiple thrones where the faithful begin to live and reign with Christ for a thousand years. This corresponds to the thrones mentioned in Daniel 7:9-14 and the giving of the kingdom to the Son of Man, that all should serve Him. This is the first resurrection.

The rest of the dead are not raised until after the thousand years are completed (see Revelation 20:4-6). At the second judgment, the dead, whether small or great, are delivered up from Death and Hades and are judged according to their works (see Revelation 20:11-15). Those not found written in the Book of Life will end up in the lake of fire—the second death. Job 14:12 says that man lies down and does not rise until the heavens are no more. Following the discussion of the great white throne judgment, Revelation 21:1-4 talks of a new heaven and a new earth and of the New Jerusalem, where there will be no more death.

Judgment begins at the house of God.

Day 19

THE LIVING AND THE DEAD

Those who believe in Him who sent Jesus shall not come into judgment, but have passed from death into life (see John 5:24). The next verse states that the (physically) dead will hear the voice of the Son of God, and those who hear will live. Jesus makes it clear that His sheep hear His voice and that they shall never perish, and neither shall anyone snatch them out of His hand (see John 10:27-30). Jesus goes on to say in John 5:28-29 that the time will come when *"all who are in the graves will hear His voice and come forth—those who have done good, to the resurrection of life, and those who have done evil, to the resurrection of condemnation."* Does not this refer to the first resurrection, namely the rapture, and secondly to the great white throne judgment?

Jesus *"will judge the living and the dead at His appearing and His kingdom"* (2 Timothy 4:1). *"To this end Christ died and rose and lived again, that He might be Lord of both the dead and the living, and each of us shall give account of himself to God"* (Romans 14:9 and 12). *"We shall all stand before the judgment seat of Christ"* (see verse 10). There will be a resurrection of the dead and a judgment of the living and the dead. First Peter 4:6 states *"For this reason the gospel was preached also to those who are dead, that they might be judged according to men in the flesh but live according to God in the spirit."* In Acts 10:42 Peter said that he had been commanded *"to preach to the people, and to testify that it is He* [Jesus] *who was ordained by God to be Judge of the living and the dead."* Paul said that *"there will be a resurrection of the dead, both of the just and the unjust"* (Acts 24:15). If we remember the less privileged, not expecting any repayment, we shall be rewarded at the resurrection of the just (see Luke 14:14).

We need to be careful what is in our hearts, as we will be condemned by our words (out of the abundance of the heart the mouth speaks) (see Matthew 12:34-37). The unforgivable act is attributing the actions of the Spirit in casting out demons to the devil and his demons (see Matthew 12:22-32 and Mark 3:28-30). A strong warning is given in Hebrews 6:4-6 to those who *"have become partakers of the Holy Spirit, and have tasted the good word of God and the powers of the age to come, if they fall away, "* that they cannot be renewed again to repentance. Also, the warning to the church of Sardis is that they will be blotted out of the Book of Life if they are spiritually dead (see Revelation 3:1-5).

Day 20

PERFECT WAY

The greatest opportunity of our lives is to be disciples of Jesus Christ, but that can only truly happen if we forsake all that we have (see Luke 14:26-33). The sign to the world that we are disciples is that we have love for one another (see John 13:34-35).

Psalm 101:6 states that whoever walks in a perfect way shall serve God. What does it mean to be perfect? Matthew 5:43-48 tells us that if we love our enemies, bless those who curse us, do good to those who hate us, and pray for those who spitefully use us and persecute us, we shall be perfect. As sons of the Father, we have seen that the anointing of God is upon us when we are persecuted. That it rains on the just and on the unjust implies that when we pray for our enemies or turn the other cheek (see Matthew 5:39), then the Spirit of Christ will rain down (see Psalm 72:6). Our bodies are temples of the Holy Spirit and we need to ensure that nothing quenches the working of the Spirit through us to bring conviction and repentance to the world (see 2 Corinthians 6:16-18). These verses quote Ezekiel 37:26, saying that God will dwell in people and walk among them. *"We are to God the fragrance of Christ,* as Paul tells us in 2 Corinthians 2:15. Is this not why Jesus was exalted to the right hand of God to be Prince and Savior and to give repentance to Israel and forgiveness of sins? (see Acts 5:31-32) There is a serious warning to us, as we walk in the world, to not defile the temple or we will be destroyed (see 1 Corinthians 3:16-17).

In Hebrews 12:15-17 we are told that Esau sought repentance but could not find it. What was the obstacle? Roots of bitterness and unforgiveness defile us and make us fall short of the grace of God. Acts 11:18 states that *"God has also granted to the Gentiles repentance to life."* It is God who draws us to repentance (see Romans 2:4). Repentance is something we cannot just do when we please. If we are to experience repentance and have a compassion for the lost, we need to remove those things that quench the move of the Spirit of God, namely bitterness, envy, unforgiveness, and being judgmental, and we need to bless those who have wronged us. We must avoid anger and negative thoughts, as they distract us from hearing the voice of God and make us less sensitive to the leading of the Spirit. If we don't forgive, then our prayers are hindered because our minds are filled with anger, resentment, and bitterness rather than with assurance of the answer. Mark 11:24-26 confirms this connection between forgiveness and answered prayer.

Day 21

GETTING BEYOND
THE "IF" WORD

If we are to pray in faith, then we need to reach a point where there is no *"if"* in prayer. Our prayer may begin with *"if,"* if we have no assurance of God's will, but it should not end with any doubt about God's will in the issue and consequently should not finish with *"if it be Your will."* To have no sure expectation of a positive response is not faith. We must get to the place where we believe our prayer has been answered—whether or not we see the manifestation. Jesus' use of the *"if"* word in the garden has often been cited as the example to follow—namely, that a prayer should end with *"if it be Your will"*—but a closer study of the text makes it clear that Jesus has no doubt about the divine will.

In Matthew 26:39, Jesus prays for the first time,

"If it is possible, let this cup pass from Me; nevertheless, not as I will, but as You will." On finding His disciples sleeping He orders them to watch and pray. A little later, in verse 42, He prays a second time, *"If this cup cannot pass away from Me unless I drink it, Your will be done."* After finding them asleep again, He prays a third time, in verse 44, saying the same words. There is no doubt expressed in the second and third prayers, but rather—a statement of fact. There is no request for His Father to remove the cup.

In Mark, Jesus prays the first time asking that if it were possible, the cup might be taken away, as all things are possible with God (see Mark 14:35). He still submits, saying, *"Nevertheless, not what I will, but what You will"* (verse 36). After finding the disciples asleep, He orders them to watch and pray, and Mark's version says He repeated the same words—though specifically which ones it is not clear. On returning, after praying the third time, He agains finds them sleeping in verse 41.

In Luke, Jesus prays, *"If it is Your will, take this cup away from Me; nevertheless not My will, but Yours, be done"* (Luke 22:42). He then prays MORE earnestly, after the angel strengthens Him, sweating blood (see verses 43-44). Is this not why the *"if"* disappeared? In verse 46, He orders His disciples to rise and pray, whereas earlier He had told them to watch and pray (in Matthew and Mark).

John 18:11 makes it clear that by the time of the betrayal, after the prayer in the garden, there is no doubt in Jesus' mind about the will of God. He rebukes Peter, saying, *"Shall I not drink the cup which My Father has given Me?"*

WHAT SHALL WE DO TO BE SAVED?

On the day of Pentecost when the people asked Peter what they should do, he said, *"Repent, and let every one of you be baptized in the name of Jesus Christ for the remission of sins; and you shall receive the gift of the Holy Spirit"* (Acts 2:38).

The first thing is repentance, which is a turning away from everything that displeases God and being truly sorry for our sins. Jesus taught repentance. The Bible states that the Lord is *"not willing that any should perish but that all should come to repentance"* (2 Peter 3:9).

Next is baptism, which is a kind of death, burial, and resurrection. However, before we are buried in the waters of baptism and have our sins washed away, we have to die. We have to die to our sins, and this involves repentance. We *"all have sinned and fall short of the glory of God"* (Romans 3:23). It may be a thought or an attitude, but we all sin every day. We may not recognize it as sin through ignorance or hardness of heart—but when the Holy Spirit does convict us, we need to turn away from it. We may not be able to turn away from it in our own strength—we need help. That help is provided by the Holy Spirit Himself—but we have to make room for the Holy Spirit to help us. We do that by dying to ourselves. How do we do that?

The Bible states that we should believe on the Lord Jesus Christ and we will be saved (see Acts 16:31). What does it mean to believe on the Lord Jesus Christ? Does it mean we believe that He existed? Does it mean we believe His words—what He said? It means much more than either of these things.

Think of a coach of a sports team who believes in one of his players. He makes a substitution and puts this player into the game. Why does he do that? Is it because he believes his player exists or believes what he said? Well, perhaps, but it is much more than that. He trusts that player to play well, and he has faith that he will have a better chance of wining the game with this player in the game.

This is how it is with the Lord Jesus Christ. We have to place our trust in Him, and that is the essence of the original Greek word meaning "to believe"—which is lost somewhat in translation. First and foremost we have to trust in Him for eternal life. We have to trust that He has already paid the penalty for our sins by His sacrifice on the cross and that there is nothing we can do in place of this to earn eternal life. Paul wrote to the Ephesians that it is by grace that we are saved through faith, and that not of ourselves; it is the gift of God—not of works, lest anyone should boast (see Ephesians 2:8-9). That is not to say we should not do good works—but we are to do them because we are saved—not in order to be saved. However, it is not just for eternal life that we need to trust Him.

We have to trust Him in every area of our lives every day. Paul said that he died daily (see 1 Corinthians 15:31). Peter wrote that we should humble ourselves under the mighty hand of God, that we should be exalted in due time, casting ALL our care on Him (see 1 Peter 5:6-7). To be led by the Spirit of God, we need to make room for the Spirit of God. We need to die to all our worries and concerns. If we simply trust in the Lord Jesus Christ to lead us and not care about the outcome one way or the other, knowing that ultimately it will work out for good, then we make room for the Spirit to lead us and the fruit of the Spirit will be manifested by supernatural peace of mind, love for the unlovable, or whatever. A good test to see if we have died to ourselves is to examine ourselves and see if there are any fears or worries in our minds. The perfect love of God casts out all fear. If we truly have submitted all our concerns to the Lord Jesus Christ, then we will not be responding to some worldly threat or fear—but to the leading of the Spirit.

After we have died and been buried in the waters of baptism, we are raised as new creations—we are literally born again. We receive eternal life when we receive the Holy Spirit. The Bible states that Jesus came to His own people and they did not receive Him—but to as many as did receive Him—He gave the power to become children of God (see John 1:11-13). It doesn't say they became children of God but that He gave them the power to become children of God. It is only those who are led by the Spirit of God who are children of God, and we can only be led by the Spirit of God if we make room for Him—by dying to our sins, to ourselves, and to our fears. Jesus and His disciples talked to two different groups of people. To those who didn't believe, they taught repentance. To those who did believe, they taught of a kingdom, a kingdom that was like a mustard seed.

When we are born again, we are babes— small seeds—but we have the potential to grow. Jesus said He came that we might have life and might have it more abundantly (see John 10:10). Sadly, many people do not seek an abundant life. The Bible states that great signs follow believers (see Mark 16:17-18).We can have a divine nature as sons of God. How fast the mustard seed grows and the how large it becomes depends on how well the seedling is watered and fed by the Word of God, prayer, and the Spirit, resulting from our dying to our sins and to ourselves.

Do you want to plant a seed and start watering it? Jesus said that unless a seed dies and falls into the ground, it has no life. He also said that he who loses his life will find it. Is there anything in your life that needs to die? Do you have any concerns about someone or something? Turn it over to God and experience the freedom. It really doesn't matter how it turns out, as it will be Spirit-led, and all things work together for good—even if you can't visualize the final outcome yet. The peace you will receive surpasses understanding—it is from the Spirit.

If you want to embark on an eternal journey, pray this prayer out loud:

Father, it is from You that come all good and perfect gifts. I pray for the greatest gift of all— the gift of eternal life in Your presence. I pray for the presence of Your Spirit of wisdom and un- derstanding, that I may clearly understand the message of the kingdom—a message that tells us that You are love and do not desire that anyone should perish—but also a message that tells us that You are just and will one day judge the world through Your Son, Jesus Christ. I pray that You would grant me an abundant measure of faith and would increase that faith, that I may believe in Your great promises.

I welcome You, Lord Jesus, into my life. I confess that I am a sinner and that I have been trusting in myself. Help me to put all my trust in You. I confess that You are Lord of my life. I believe You have been raised from the dead and have paid the penalty for all my sins. Help me to follow You all the days of my life.

Father, it is written in Your Word: *"He who believes in the Son of God has the witness in himself"* (1 John 5:10). May Your Spirit confirm to my spirit that I am a child of God and grant me the assurance that I am growing daily in Your everlasting kingdom.

In Jesus' name. Amen.